THE BLACK SOLDIER

Co-edited by Jay David and Elaine Crane

The Black Soldier
Living Black in White America

Co-edited by Jay David

To Be A Black Woman (with Mel Watkins)
Growing Up African (with Helise Harrington)

Edited by Jay David

Growing Up Black

THE BLACK SOLDIER

*From the American
Revolution to Vietnam*

*Edited by
Jay David and Elaine Crane*

William Morrow and Company, Inc., New York 1971

Printed in the United States of America.
Library of Congress Catalog Card Number 72-151931

Grateful acknowledgment is made for permission to reprint the following:

Selection from *Proud Shoes*, by Pauli Murray, copyright © 1956 by Pauli Murray and reprinted with his permission.

Selection from *The Buffalo Soldiers: A Narrative of the Negro Cavalry in the West*, by William H. Leckie. Copyright 1967 by the University of Oklahoma Press.

Selection from *From Harlem to the Rhine*, by Arthur Little. Copyright 1936 by Covici Friede, Inc. Used by permission of Crown Publishers, Inc.

Selection from *Yes I Can*, by Sammy Davis, Jr., and Jane and Burt Boyar. Copyright © 1965 by Sammy Davis, Jr., Jane Boyar and Burt Boyar. Reprinted by permission of Farrar, Straus & Giroux, Inc.

Selection from *A Choice of Weapons*, by Gordon Parks. Copyright © 1965, 1966 by Gordon Parks. Reprinted by permission of Harper & Row, Publishers, Inc.

Selection from *Ebony Brass*, by Jesse J. Johnson, Lt. Col., Retired. Copyright © 1967 by Jesse J. Johnson and reprinted with his permission.

Selection from *This Is My Country Too*, by John A. Williams. Copyright © 1964, 1965 by John A. Williams. Reprinted by permission of The World Publishing Company.

When the Black G.I. Comes Back from Vietnam, by Sol Stern. Copyright © 1968 by The New York Times Company. Reprinted by permission.

Selections from *G.I. Diary*, by David Parks. Copyright © 1968 by David M. Parks. Reprinted by permission of Harper & Row, Publishers, Inc.

From Dakto to Detroit: Death of a Troubled Hero, by Jon Nordheimer. Copyright © 1971 by The New York Times Company. Reprinted by permission.

2   3   4   5   75   74   73   72

CONTENTS

"Marching Song of the First Arkansas"
by Lindley Miller

Sung to the tune of "John Brown's Body," the "Marching Song of the First Arkansas" was the fighting song of the First Arkansas Colored Regiment of the Union Army. It was written in 1863 by Captain Lindley Miller, a member of a New York regiment and later commander of this Negro regiment. He called it "a good song to fight with." The song was widely popular among Negro troops during the war.

Oh, we're the bully soldiers of the "First of Arkansas,"
We are fighting for the Union, we are fighting for the law,
We can hit a Rebel further than a white man ever saw,
    As we go marching on.

Chorus:
Glory, glory, hallelujah,
Glory, glory, hallelujah,
Glory, glory, hallelujah,
As we go marching on.

See, there above the center, where the flag is waving
  bright,
We are going out of slavery, we're bound for freedom's
  light;
We mean to show Jeff Davis how the Africans can fight,
      As we go marching on!

We have done with hoeing cotton, we have done with
  hoeing corn,
We are colored Yankee soldiers, now, as sure as you are
  born;
When the masters hear us yelling, they'll think it's
  Gabriel's horn,
      As it went sounding on.

They will have to pay us wages, the wages of their sin,
They will have to bow their foreheads to their colored
  kith and kin,
They will have to give us house-room, or the roof shall
  tumble in!
      As we go marching on.

They said, "Now colored brethren, you shall be forever
  free,
From the first of January, eighteen hundred sixty-three."
We heard it in the river going rushing to the sea,
      As it went sounding on.

Father Abraham has spoken and the message has been
  sent,
The prison doors he opened, and out the prisoners went,
To join the sable army of the "African descent,"
      As we go marching on.

Then fall in, colored brethren, you'd better do it soon,
Don't you hear the drum a-beating the Yankee Doodle
tune?
We are with you now this morning, we'll be far away at
noon,
    As we go marching on.

INTRODUCTION

The black soldier has always carried on a two-front war. The first has been against America's common enemy and the second against the racism of his own country.

During the Revolution freedman and slave took up the cause of independence despite a ruling which excluded slaves on the somewhat incongruous grounds that their service would be "inconsistent with the principles that are to be supported." And while Negro soldiers distinguished themselves in the early battles of the War for Independence, movement was afoot to rid the army of all black men. On November 12, 1775, General Washington, motivated partially by prejudice and partially by fear of arming the blacks, issued an order instructing recruiters not to enlist Negroes. Whatever his reasons, Washington nonetheless found himself in an awkward position when the news arrived that the British army was eagerly welcoming free blacks and runaway slaves. As Negroes, both slaves and freedmen, began to flock toward the British lines, the American army was forced to modify its position. Owners were given bounties to provide slaves for the duration of the war. In some cases, slaves turned soldier were promised their freedom at the end of the war, and their masters were compensated at the going rate for human flesh.

Approximately 300,000 Americans fought against England during the Revolution, and, of that number, about 5,000 were Negroes. While the overwhelming percentage of blacks lived in the South, most Negro soldiers came from northern states. There were very few black units.

Integration in the army was virtually complete. This would not happen again for nearly two centuries.

Most slaves were not given their promised freedom at the end of the Revolution—or for that matter, at the end of the War of 1812—as James Roberts attests. It would be fifty years before the slave would be reluctantly granted permission to die for freedom. In the meantime, however, there were slaves who were not content to wait. Gabriel Prosser, Nat Turner, and Denmark Vesey were among those who organized their own armies in pursuit of freedom.

From the very beginning of the Civil War, northern blacks begged to enlist and were refused. It was a white man's war, they were told, and it was being fought to preserve the Union. It was not until abolition became inseparably linked with the restoration of the Union that the North seriously considered raising Negro troops. After 1862 free Negroes and emancipated slaves played an increasingly vital role in the Union war effort. More than 200,000 Negroes—in separate units—fought in the Union army and navy. They were crucial to a Union victory.

After the war, black men were called to fight red men in the West and, still not convinced of the Negro's soldiering ability, white men in Washington made it as difficult as possible. The same inequalities which existed in civilian life manifested and magnified themselves in the army.

As late as World War I, Negroes were barred altogether from the marines, and were permitted to serve in the navy only in the most menial capacities. In the army, however, they served in nearly every branch, although, as usual, in segregated units. There was a great deal of discrimination in the army and the civilian agencies that serviced it. Blacks were continuously insulted by their white officers and men from other units. Friction grew between the military police and the Negro soldier. Most black soldiers agreed that they were better treated in Europe than in the States.

Approximately 500,000 Negroes served overseas in World War II. Although discrimination in the service still kept pace with civilian life, by the end of the war black men were serving in every branch of the military in integrated units. The discontent at home during the war years, however, manifested itself in a series of race riots. Great migrations from the South had resulted in large Negro ghettos in major cities of the North. Blacks, finding it increasingly difficult to get along peaceably, and resentful of their minimal share of the benefits that came from the huge war effort, exploded. The most serious race riot of the war years took place in Detroit in 1943. At the end of the rioting twenty-five Negroes and nine whites were dead; half a million dollars' worth of property had been destroyed. By the end of the war, black soldiers were openly asking themselves why they should fight to preserve the injustices they suffered.

It was left to Harry Truman to put an American president squarely on the side of equality in the armed forces. On July 26, 1948, he signed Executive Order 9981 which created the President's Committee on Equality of Treatment and Opportunity in the Armed Services. After two years the committee reported that some reduction in the inequalities existing in the Armed Services had been achieved. In 1951 there were 200,000 Negro soldiers serving in 385 all-Negro units. By September, 1953, at the end of the Korean War, only 88 all-Negro units remained in the army. These units accounted for only five percent of the Negro enlisted men.

Ironically, although blacks are now freely accepted into

the American armed forces, they are the victims of a far greater discrimination than ever before practiced. In 1966 there were 22,000 Negroes in Vietnam, some fifteen percent of the total United States commitment there. During the year, 22½ percent of all army troops killed in action were blacks. These statistics suggest two things. First, since Negroes compose only ten percent of the total American population, there were proportionately more Negroes in the service than in civilian life, and second, a greater number of blacks than whites were being sent to combat and danger zones. There has been a conscious effort on the part of the current Administration to have black military participation in Southeast Asia more accurately reflect the percentage of blacks in the American population as a whole. Interestingly enough, the total percentage of Negroes in the armed forces in Southeast Asia has dropped because of a precipitous decline in the numbers entering the army and navy. The marines and air force actually show an increase in black enlistment since 1966.

Despite the government's efforts to lower the percentage of blacks engaged in combat, now more than ever before, black Americans are critical of America's role in this Far Eastern War, saying that the millions spent in Vietnam could be put to better use at home. Some, like John Sumrall, have refused to serve altogether. As the war gained in disfavor and black aspirations reached new peaks in the states, racial unrest heightened in Vietnam. Within integrated fighting units black soldiers imposed segregation. The presence of Black power salutes and black flags have been some indication of the defiant racial pride which has burst forth. White provocations have caused both riots and near riots. When Martin Luther King was killed fiery crosses burned in Danang and Cam

Ranh Bay. And racial conflict is not confined to Vietnam. Okinawa and Germany have seen their share.

For two hundred years the black soldier has fought for his own personal freedom as well as for his country. It is no longer a question of proving ability; the black soldier has proved his heroism. Today the issues are acceptance as a human being and an American citizen and being granted the dignity and the privileges those identities imply.

> *Jay David*
> *Elaine Crane*
> *1971*

1

FROM

The Narrative of James Roberts, Soldier in the Revolutionary War

by James Roberts
(1753–?)

The story of James Roberts is similar to that of many Negroes who fought in the Revolution. While we know of Roberts only through his own words, the valor of such patriots as Peter Salem, Salem Poor, Caesar Brown and Prince Hall, among others, are well recorded in contemporary documents. It is said that Peter Salem earned a great moral victory for his comrades by killing the British Major John Pitcairn, at the Battle of Bunker Hill.

Roberts takes us through the French and Indian Wars, the Revolution, and the War of 1812, giving us in turn a humorous portrait of Lord Cornwallis and an unusual glimpse of the great democrat, Andrew Jackson.

I was born on the Eastern Shore of Maryland, in the year of our Lord 1753, in a state of slavery, and belonged to Francis De Shields. He was a colonel in Washington's army. I was with him in the war, and helped to scalp and kill many Indians, which I now exceedingly regret, as they were innocent and defenceless, and were fast tending to a condition not much better than my own. I was with him through the whole course of the Revolutionary War. At the battle of White Haven, I fought in Washington's army; after that, at the battle of Roanoke river. There human blood ran down in torrents, till the waters of the river were red as crimson. The next battle in which I was engaged was at Ragged Point, on Dorset county river; next, Vienna Ferry; thence to Cambridge. From there we retreated to Prince Anne, at that time called Yorktown, where Lord Cornwallis was surrounded by Washington, to whom Cornwallis surrendered his sword. When he did so he said, "I am no more Lord *Corn*wallis, I am *Cob*-wallis, with the *corn* shelled off."

Then the seven years' war with Britain soon closed, and Washington became President of the United States. My master was the Vice President * and I was there in Philadelphia when Washington took his seat. Five years after, my master died in Philadelphia, and I returned with his horses and carriage to the Eastern Shore of Maryland, with five hundred dollars in the carriage, which no one in the world knew anything of but myself. I delivered horses, carriage, money and myself to my master's family, prompted to do so at that time by a sense of honor and justice. The whole of which, myself included, with the six horses, fine coach and money, was worth at least three thousand seven hundred dollars, all of which I might have taken to myself and made my escape to some other country; for no one had any control over either myself, the horses, carriage or money, or knew anything about my leaving Philadelphia. I was acquainted with every part of the country, and was well known everywhere, so that I could have made up any tale I pleased, and passed off. And I will now confess, that, could I have foreseen what heart-sickening ills awaited me in the future, I

---

* Here Roberts' memory fails him. John Adams, Washington's Vice President, was a violent opponent of slavery and could never have been Roberts' "master."

should have been strongly tempted to make my way to Canada, which I might have done, for I knew where and how to have gone into that country. Had I done so, and appropriated to myself the horses, carriage and money, I should not have been overpaid for my unrequited labor and services. But honor, justice, and the hope of being set free, with my wife and four little ones, prompted me to return home.

But, instead of freedom, I was, soon after my return, sold to William Ward, separated from my wife and children, taken to New Orleans, and sold at auction sale to Calvin Smith, a planter in Louisiana, for fifteen hundred dollars. And now will commence the statement of the payment of my wages, for all of my fighting and suffering in the Revolutionary War for the liberty of this ungrateful, illiberal country, to me and to my race.

Calvin Smith took me home to his plantation, or, more appropriately, his slaughter-house of human beings, as will appear in this narrative. To initiate me, as he said, into the profound mysteries of that part of the country, he ordered the overseer to give me nine-and-thirty lashes before I had done a stroke of work. He then took from me all of my clothes which I had worn in Philadelphia, and some of my regimentals which I wished to keep as memorials of revolutionary times, and gave me instead but a bare breech-clout, and sent me into the field to work.

General Jackson, in order to prepare to meet Packenham, the British General, in the contest at New Orleans, came into our section of the country, enlisting soldiers. He came to Calvin Smith's, and made a bargain with him to enlist five hundred negroes. Jackson came into the field, chose out the ones he wanted, and then addressed us thus: "Had you not as soon go into the battle and fight, as to stay here in the cotton field, dying and never die? If you will go, and the battle is fought and the victory gained on Israel's side, you shall be free." This short speech seemed to us like divine revelation, and it filled our souls with buoyant expectations. Hardships, of whatever kind or however severe, vanished into vapor at the sound of freedom, and I made Jackson this reply: that, in hope of freedom we would "run through a troop and leap over a wall;" that I had as well go there and die for an old sheep as for a lamb. We were taken to Washington, in Louisiana, and drilled. Jackson again told us that we should be free after the battle. Calvin Smith said to Jackson, "encourage your soldiers by telling them they shall be free; then they will fight the more valiantly for freedom." He said to Jackson: "If there are not enough of blacks in place of my sons, go to the Springfield plantation and get as many more. If the negroes should go and get killed, they are paid for; but, if my children should go and get killed, they cannot be replaced." For what man will not think more of his child than he will of a negro? and a negro has got more ambition to fight than a white man. Captain Brown, of Tennessee, said to Smith: "I glory in your spunk; let us have as many negroes as you can spare, for we are sure that those negroes you give us will gain the victory."

Captain Brown mustered and drilled us, taking us through the evolutions: how to wheel to the right and left, from a single file to a double platoon; to march and wheel with the left foot foremost; to charge, cook and fire, ease arms, &c. Being satisfied as to our proficiency in military tactics, we prepared to start to New Orleans.

We took up our march from Natchez, and traveled the whole distance, three hundred miles by land, on foot.

Every man had a sack and musket. When we came to the swamps in Louisiana, the water in some places was knee deep, with thick green scum over it, which we had to remove before we could get to the stinking water. At night we made little piles of brush, wood and grass for our beds. Here the musquitos, gallinippers and red-belly snakes, at night when we laid down, contested with one another, over our bodies, which should get the greatest share of blood before morning. We had to sleep with one eye, keep awake with the other, in order to keep off the snakes, which we would thrust away a dozen times a night, when they would be crawling over us.

A number of the white Kentuckians died in the swamps from drinking the poisonous water. Jackson addressed them to this effect: It is a pity that you white devils did not stay at your homes. The negroes are no trouble at all. It would have been far better for us to have had no whites, for there is not a day or night passes that we do not have to dig a hole and bury five or six of you. It will be better for us to discharge you all and take you no farther.

In one week after leaving Natchez, we arrived in sight of New Orleans. We marched forward till we came in sight of the British army, and the first view of it was very impressive indeed. The British soldiers wore large, brilliant steel breast-plates, steel caps and steel covers on their arms up to the shoulders. The sun shining on these plates, and on their bright swords and spears, gave an appearance that inspired in me a dread and fear that is not easily described. Jackson said to us: "Don't be discouraged. Take the second look at them; they are but men like yourselves. Courage will overcome your fears and dread." We then marched next to the marsh and formed a single file. Then Jackson and Packenham the

British general met and held a consultation. Then each general counted the number of the other's army. Packenham had ten to Jackson's one. Packenham asked Jackson if he was ready for operations. Jackson replied, he had not consulted his mind. Packenham said, I will give you two days to make up your mind.

Now Jackson consulted what was best to be done. In the meantime Packenham drew up his army along the water side, and remained there two days. There was in Jackson's army a colored soldier named Pompey, who gave Jackson the first idea about the *cotton-bag fort,* and superintended the construction of it. We engaged in making it, and it was completed in the latter part of the second day. The cotton-bags were so placed as to leave port holes for three muskets to point through each.

On the third day, Packenham, buoyant with hope and flush with ambition, came towards our camp and demanded an interview with Jackson. The two generals met, in full view of the two armies, and held a consultation again. Packenham asked Jackson if he was ready for operations now, who replied that he was, and then asked Packenham how he liked his wooly-headed boys. Packenham said he had rather fight ten white men to their one, for, when they begin, there is no rule with them to stop but death. Then, said Jackson, say the word, and the wool flies. This day, said the exulting Packenham, I will either eat my dinner in the city of New Orleans, or in h--l! Poor, ill-fated man! little did he know that, within two hours from that moment, he was to fall by the hand of one of the wooly-headed boys.

Each general returned to his respective army, and in twenty minutes the British fired. They fired three rounds, and the fourth we opened upon them. Here they began to throw shells into our fort, and had they continued to do so for some time, there is no doubt but victory would have been easy to them. But Packenham, who headed his army, impatient to carry everything by main force, doubting nothing as to his ability to take the fort in a short period, rushed forward in quick evolutions; and, as they came, we felled them like grass before the scythe. Platoon after platoon lay like scattered hail upon the ground. Packenham seeing this, and observing the rapid loss of his men, marched them single file up to our fort. He himself mounted the wall, encouraging his men in the most energetic manner. And here, at this point of the battle he might have succeeded, had he exercised some discretion. Instead of ordering the bags to be pushed inside next to us, he ordered them to be pulled outside, which entangled his men, and while in that entanglement we slew them by the scores, and piled them by hundreds upon the bags as they endeavored to climb over them. While this was going on in the main body of our fort, the left wing of the fort gave way, which brought us and the British in immediate contact, with the broad-sword, and they fell before us like grass before the scythe. At this point I lost the fore finger of my left hand, and received a deep wound on my head from a British sword. After that I took the fellow's head off, and five more of his fellow soldiers. Packenham at that moment was shot from the wall, and in two minutes the red flag was hauled down and the white one hoisted, the battle ceased and victory declared on our side. Jackson, who, during the battle, had taken a stand at some distance, ordering his men by an aide-de-camp, came up to the line and gave us three cheers, and observing me to be all over bloody, asked me what was the matter with me. I told him not anything, for I had not yet discovered the loss of my finger, nor the wound upon my head. He said, "you have lost one of your fingers and received a deep wound upon your head; go to the hospital and have your wounds dressed." I did so, and returned to him, and asked him to let me go on the side of the British and see the slain. He said, "go where you please; the ground is free to you all, and all yours." I went and saw the slain lying, for one quarter of a mile, as thick as they could lie upon the ground, and I walked shoe deep in blood that distance and back. Some of the poor fellows were dead, some dying, some half dead, some cut in half and still living, and, as I passed by them, they grated their teeth at me, and made efforts to come at me. We were ordered to bury the slain of the British. We dug trenches and pulled them in with our grab-hooks, whether they were dead or still breathing. We were ordered to cover up the devils whether dead or alive, which we did, and tramped them down with our feet, into the blood and water knee deep. We then buried our own dead, putting them into coffins and burying them in the city.

In that battle some sixty or seventy or more of the colored men were killed, of whom no account whatever was ever taken in the details of the war, although they were, without doubt, as Jackson himself acknowledged, the instrumental cause of the victory. Such black ingratitude deserves the deepest reprehension. A savage would have been more grateful. Had we thus fought in the army of the cruel Turks, we should have received that applause which such merit deserved. But this inhuman neglect was left for Jackson's reprehensible duplicity.

Having buried our dead, we returned back to the fort. The British had by this time got a pipe of rum from the city, to preserve the body of Packenham, into which the body was put and headed up.

We formed a line, took our arms, and serenaded the

battleground. Gabriel Winton, with his two colored boys, conducted the music. One played the fife, and the other the bass drum. One was named Spot, and the other Wot. These boys excelled, in this department of necessary warfare, any that were upon the battle-ground. The battle was now fully closed. Next day morning, we put all our guns away in the ammunition house, and Jackson ordered them to be unloaded, to serve a wicked end he had in view, which I shall presently notice. The next day morning, being the second day after the battle, we came to get our guns, to march. We had power to put our guns away, but none to take them out of the ammunition house. A white man handed them out to us. We formed a line and marched down Fourth Street, up Porass Street, where the ladies through the windows waved their handkerchiefs and complimented Jackson on his success and victory. Here we formed a line in the presence of thousands. Jackson came riding along and said, "Well done, my brave boys, I will give you the praise; you have fought like bulldogs, and wallowed in your blood;" then, addressing the crowd, he said, "if you ever want a battle fought, get the negro's ebenezer up, and he will run through a troop and leap over a wall. They are the best nation to fight in existence." Again turning to his colored soldiers, he said, "Now, behave yourselves well, and go home to your masters." I then said, A word to you, General, if you please: have you time to speak a word to me? "What is the word you wish to speak to me?" I asked him if he did not promise me my freedom, if that battle was fought and victory gained? He replied, "I did, but I took your master's word, as he told me. You are not my property, and I cannot take another man's property and set it free." My answer was, You can use your influence with our master, and have us set free. He replied thus: "If I were to hire you my horse, could you sell it without my leave? You are another man's property, and I have not money sufficient to buy all of you, and set you free." At that moment I cocked my gun; but there being no priming in it, I bit off a piece of cartridge, and, going to prime it, I for the first time discovered it was not loaded. Had my gun been loaded, doubtless Jackson would have been a dead man in a moment. There was no fear in my soul, at that time, of anything, neither man, death, nor mortal. The war-blood was up. I had just two days before cut off the heads of six brave Englishmen, and Jackson's life, at that moment, appeared no more to me than theirs. It was well for him that he took the precaution to have our guns unloaded when in the ammunition house. His guilty conscience smote him, and told him he was doing us a great piece of injustice, in promising us, by the most solemn protestation, that we should be free if the victory were gained. I would then have shot him dead a thousand times, if that could have been done. My soul was stirred in me, and maddened to desperation, to think that we had placed our lives in such imminent peril, through the persuasions of such false-heartedness, and now told to go back home to our masters!

Jackson asked me if I contended for freedom. I said I did. He said, "I think you are very presumptuous." I told him, the time had come for us to claim our rights. He said, "You promised me that you would fight manfully." I did, sir, and now is the time for me to claim the benefit of the promise you made me. I did fight manfully and gained the victory, now where is my freedom? He replied, as he had nothing else to reply, "You are a day too late; and if you are not willing to go home, I will put you in confinement, and send for your master; he will take you home; you seem to be the hardest among the whole crew."

Some of the whites standing round said, "He ought to be shot." Now, just think of that! Two days before, I had, with my fellow soldiers, saved their city from fire and massacre, and their wives and children from blood and burning, now, "he ought to be shot!" simply for contending for my freedom, which, both my master and Jackson had solemnly before high heaven promised, before I left home.

Captain Brown, however, who knew something at least of the value of our services, or in some degree appreciated them, said, "No, he shall not be shot. You should not have promised him his liberty," addressing Jackson, "if you did not intend to fulfil your word. All negroes are not fools," said he; "some of them have as good sense as you or I."

I said, as for my part, I have sense enough to know there has been great falsehood practiced in this whole transaction; and had I had the least anticipation of it, I would never have come here to put my life in peril for such a cause.

Captain Brown said, pointing significantly at me, "That Jim, who is contending for his rights, is no fool. Some of the negroes you can scare; but there is no scare in him."

Then Jackson said, "We will march to the Kentucky Tavern, on Water Street." Having arrived there, he told the landlord to give us as much liquor as we could drink. The most of them drank heartily and freely, while others drank nothing at all, being sorely oppressed with grief, and saying that they would rather die than go back to the plantation, where misery only awaited them on their return from the glorious battle-field of the country's defence. I told Jackson, when he insisted on my drinking, I was now going back to die in the cottonfield, and that

I would not drink a drop. I told him I did not like such base falsehood as was now to be practiced upon us. I was not such a fool as to be paid with a glass of liquor for such meritorious services.

Now Jackson commenced his speech about the negroes. "Never," said he, "suffer negroes to have arms; if you do, they will take the country. Suffer them to have no kind of weapons over ten inches long. Never allow them to have a piece of paper with any writing on it whatever. You must examine your slaves very closely, for the time is coming when the slave will get light; and if ever his mind is enlightened on the subject of freedom, you cannot keep him. One slave bought from the East will ruin a multitude of those raised here. Before a slave of mine should go free, I would put him in a barn and burn him alive. Gentlemen, take me at my word; for if you do not, you will be sorry for it before many years. Never arm another set of colored people. We have fooled them now, but never trust them again; they will not be fooled again with this example before them. If you do, you will repent of it but once. Look," said he, "at Pompey, whom we ordered to be shot on the battle-ground, because he would not stop fighting, even after the battle had ended, till he was shot down. Look, I entreat you, at his indomitable spirit; he had the disposition of the bull-dog."

Such was Jackson's speech in our presence. Why was not this speech published in the history of that war? No mention is made of it whatever. Such monstrous deception and villainy could not, of course, be allowed to disgrace the pages of history, and blacken the character of a man who wanted the applause and approbation of his country. But we here drag it to light, that it may be held up to universal execration by all lovers of right, justice and freedom.

Night now drew on, when we were ordered back to the

calaboose, for safe-keeping till morning. Mr. Seymour Johnson, the keeper of the calaboose, said, "Not so; they have done no crime. My order is, to take them back to the tavern, and board them there till the morning."

Here was another act of intolerable injustice to soldiers just from the field of victory and glory, but now to be incarcerated in a criminal jail!

The next morning the steamer *Walk-in-the-Water* was to leave New Orleans for Natchez, and our passage was engaged on her. We marched down to the boat, followed by an immense crowd of pedestrians, and ladies and gentlemen in carriages. Having arrived at the river, and halted, the ladies made this speech to Jackson:

"GENERAL: It is wrong, decidedly wrong, to treat these men so. You took the martial law into your own hands, for which you was fined a large sum, and which sum we ladies paid for you; and now, we wish for our remuneration—nothing more than the freedom of these men, by your interceding with their masters for them. Will you promise us to do it?"

Jackson replied, "I cannot,"—and the boat started.

When we reached Natchez, Calvin Smith was there ready to receive his hands.

"Well, Jim," said he, "you did not get killed."

"No, sir, I did not."

"Then you can raise more cotton and sugar yet."

I said, "I think I ought to be free."

"I'll give you freedom on your back."

"I am only contending, master, for what you promised me. You ought never to have promised to set me free, if you had no mind to do it. You promised me if I would go down and fight, in the place of your children, I should be free."

"When I get you home I'll give you freedom."

He took me home and delivered me to the overseer, and gave him a letter from Jackson, stating how I had contended with him in New Orleans for my freedom. "Now, therefore, scourge him severely." The overseer asked how many lashes he should give me. "Give him one hundred; it will bring him to his feeling." His oldest son Stephen came up and said: "Father, it is wrong; you ought never to have promised it to him. It is wrong to whip him for what you promised to do for him." By that means I got clear of my whipping. Stephen ordered the overseer not to whip me.

The overseer then took my clothes from me, and clothed me, who had just saved the country from destruction, in a breech-clout, and sent me into the field to work.

2

The Trial Record of Denmark Vesey
(1767–1822)

While many of the facts pertaining to slave revolts are clouded in obscurity, one fact remains indisputably clear: black soldiers exploded the southern contention that all slaves were docile.

Denmark Vesey was born a slave in 1767 but purchased his freedom in 1800 with winnings from a lottery. Vesey was aware of the storm of revolution in Haiti in the early nineteenth century, and this undoubtedly gave impetus to his movement. For four years following 1818 Vesey preached revolution to any who would listen, and many did. By 1822 his army numbered in the thousands, and he planned to kill every white person in Charleston, South Carolina. The most important element in Vesey's undertaking was surprise and, because of the sheer numbers involved, this proved impossible. Hundreds of blacks were arrested before the actual insurrection got underway, and thirty-five of the conspirators, including Vesey, were hanged. During the trial most of the leaders obeyed Peter Poyas' admonition, "Do not open your lips! Die silent, as you shall see me do."

THE TRIAL OF PETER, a Negro man, the property of Mr. James Poyas—Mr. Poyas with Robert Bentham, Esq. as his counsel attending.

Evidence

Witness No. 5   A Negro man gave the following evidence: I know Peter, he belongs to Mr. James Poyas. In May last Peter and myself met in Legare Street, at the corner of Lambol Street, when the following conversation took place. He asked me the news—I replied none that I know of. He said by George we can't live so—I replied how will we do. He said we can do very well; if you can find anyone to assist us will you join. I asked him how do you mean—he said, why to break the yoke. I replied I don't know. He asked me suppose you were to hear that the whites were going to kill you would you defend yourself—I replied I'd try to escape. He asked have you lately seen Denmark Vesey, and has he spoken to you particularly—I said no. Well then said he that's all now, but call at the shop tomorrow after knocking off work and I will tell you more—we then parted. I met him the next day according to appointment, when he said to me, we intend to see if we can't do something for ourselves, we can't live so. I asked him where he would get men—he said we'll find them fast enough, we have got enough—we expect men from country and town. But how said I will you manage it—why we will give them notice said he, and they will march down and camp round the city. But what said I will they do for arms—he answered they will find arms enough, they will bring down their hoes, axes, &c. I said that won't do to fight with here—he said stop, let us get candidates from town with arms, and we will then take the Guard House and Arsenal in town, the Arsenal on the Neck and the upper Guard House, and supply the country people with arms. How said I will you approach these Arsenals for they are guarded— yes said he, I know that, but what are those guards, one man here and one man there, we won't let a man pass

before us. Well said I but how will the black people from
the country and those from the Islands know when you
are to begin; or how will you get the town people together—why said he we will have *prayer meetings at night
and there notify them* when to start and as the clock
strikes 12 all must move—But said I, the whites in the
back country, Virginia, when they hear the news will
turn to and kill you all, and besides you may be betrayed.
Well said he what of that, if one gets hanged we will rise
at that minute. We then left his shop and walked towards
Broad Street, when he said *I want you to take notice of
all the shops and stores in town with arms in them, take
down the numbers and give them to me.* I said I will see
to it and then we parted. About the 1st June I saw in the
public papers a statement that the white people were
going to build Missionary Houses for the blacks, which
I carried and showed to Peter and said to him, you see
the good they are going to do for us—when he said, what
of that, have you not heard that on the 4th July the
whites are going to create a false alarm of fire, and every
black that comes out will be killed in order to thin them.
Do you think that they would be so barbarous said I. Yes
said he I do; I fear they have knowledge of an army from
Santo Domingo, and they would be right to do it, to prevent us from joining that army if it should march towards
this land. I was then very much alarmed—we then parted
and I saw no more of him until (the Guards were very
strict) about a fortnight ago. At that time I saw Peter
and Ned Bennett standing and talking together at the
corner of Lambol and Legare Streets—they crossed over
and met me by Mrs. Myles, and Ned Bennett said to me,
did you hear what those boys were taken up for the other
day. I replied No, but some say 'twas for stealing. Ned
asked me if I was sure I had never said anything to the

whites about what Peter Poyas had spoken to me about—
I replied No—says Peter you never did—No I answered
—says Ned to me how do you stand—at which, I struck
the tree box with my knuckles and said, as firm as this
box, I'll never say one word against you. Ned then smiled
and nodded his head and said, that will do, when we all
separated. Last Tuesday or Wednesday week Peter said
to me you see my lad how the white people have got to
windward of us—you won't said I be able to do anything.
O yes said he we will, by George, we are obliged to—he
said all down this way ought to meet and have a collec-
tion to purchase powder. What said I is the use of powder, the whites can fire three times to our once—he said
but 'twill *be such a dead time of night they won't know
what is the matter, and our Horse Companies will go
about the streets and prevent the whites from assembling.*
I asked him where will you get horses—why said he there
are many butcher boys with horses, and there are the
public Livery Stables, where we have several candidates
and the waiting men belonging to the white people of
the Horse Companies will be told to take away their master's horses. He asked me if my master was not a horse-
man—I said yes. Has he not got arms in his house—I answered yes. Can't they be got at—I said yes—then said he
'tis good to have them. I asked him what was the plan—
why said he after we have taken the Arsenal and Guard
Houses, then we will set the town on fire in different
places, and as the whites come out we will slay them; if
we were to set fire to the town first, the man in the steeple
would give the alarm too soon—*I am the Captain said he,
to take the lower Guard House and Arsenal.* But, I replied, when you are coming up the sentinel will give the
alarm—he said he would advance a little distance ahead,
and if he could only get *a grip at his throat he was a gone*

man, for his sword was very sharp; he had sharpened it and had made it so sharp it had cut his finger, which he showed me. As to the Arsenal on the Neck he said that is gone as sure as fate, *Ned Bennett would manage that with the people from the country, and the people between Hibben's Ferry and Santee would land and take the upper Guard House.* I then said, then this thing seems true. My man, said he, God has a hand in it, we have been meeting for four years and are not yet betrayed. I told him I was afraid after all of the white people from the back country and Virginia. He said that the blacks would collect so numerous *from the country* we need not fear the whites from other parts, for when we have once got the city we can keep them all out. He asked if I had told my boys—I said no—then he said you should do it, for Ned Bennett has his people pretty well ranged; but said he take care and don't mention it to those waiting men who receive *presents of old coats from their masters or they'll betray us;* I will speak to them. We then parted and I have not conversed with him. He said the rising was to take place last Sunday night (16th June)—*that any of the colored people who said a word about this matter would be killed by the others—the little man who can't be killed, shot, or taken* is named Jack, a Gullah Negro. Peter said there was a French company in town *of 300 men fully armed*—that he was to see Monday Gell about expediting the rising. I know that Mingo went often to Mr. Paul's to see Edwin, but don't know if he spoke with William. *Peter said he had a sword* and I ought to get one—he said he had a letter from the country, I think from St. Thomas', from a Negro man who belonged to the Captain of a Militia Company, who said he could easily get the key of the house where the Company's arms were put after muster, and take them all out and help in that way. This business originates altogether with the *African Congregation* in which Peter is a leader. When Bennett's Ned asked about those taken up, he alluded particularly to Mr. Paul's William, and asked me if I had said anything to him about it.

The owner of Witness No. 5, testified as follows: My servant bears a good character. His general conduct is good. He was raised up in my family, and I would place my life in his hands.

3

FROM
Proud Shoes
by Pauli Murray
(1910–   )

*Less than fifty years ago historian W. E. Woodward re-
flected the consensus opinion that "the American Negroes are the only people in the history of the world . . .
that ever became free without any effort of their own.
. . ." Nothing could be further from the truth. If Denmark Vesey's army was aborted in its attempt to achieve
freedom, General Grant's was not, and Grant's army had
over 200,000 Negroes fighting in it.*

*At the beginning of the war, however, Lincoln refused
to raise Negro troops. For the first two years he attempted
to placate the border states by not permitting the enlistment of blacks in the Union army. Thus, when Negroes
quickly offered their services to the Union cause, they
were summarily rejected. Undaunted, runaway slaves and
free blacks continued to press for military service, and in
the meantime did whatever they could to assist the war
effort. Such a person was Pauli Murray's grandfather, described by her in the following selection.*

The Civil War was the only war of importance in our
family. We had no menfolk enlisted in the Spanish-Amer-
ican War and World War I to relate personal memories

and make them real to us, but the Civil War was as close to us as if it had been fought yesterday. Grandfather's memories and modest trophies kept the Yankee cause shining brightly in our home.

If the Rebels had their monuments and symbols, we had ours. Under Grandfather's bed lay his musket and rusty saber, his bayonet and cavalry pistol, an 1856 Springfield model. The saber's blade was as dull as its back and the firearms had not been loaded for years, but their lack of utility made them no less significant in our eyes. They were symbols of courage and of a tradition which made us stand tall. When other children boasted, "My father is a preacher," or "My father has an automobile," I'd counter with, "My grandfather was a soldier in the Union and fought for freedom." Few of my playmates could match that!

There were other symbols too, which miraculously survived three quarters of a century, not as impressive to me in those years as the musket and saber, but which were to serve as windows through which I later glimpsed Grandfather's youth. Like many young men of his time, he kept a diary during and after the Civil War, closely scribbled in tiny notebooks and meaningless to me in childhood. For years Aunt Pauline kept them carefully buried underneath old letters and papers in her top desk drawer. She claimed that in a spell of being helpful while she was away from home one day, I cleaned house and dumped some of Grandfather's letters and diaries down the well along with old shoes, tin cans and bottles to help fill it up. I could not deny it, for only two small volumes of the diaries are left, but fortunately the Fitzgeralds had remarkably long and accurate memories.

Grandfather never got over his soldiering. You could always get him to talk about the Civil War, and while he

was not a boastful man he'd say with considerable emphasis, "Your Uncle Richard drove mules for the Union, but
I was a sailor and a soldier." When I'd lead him about
the town, he'd press hard on my shoulder when he
wanted me to get in step, and, having shorter legs than
his, I'd have to skip now and then to keep the rhythm.
His Presbyterian soul frowned upon such frivolities as
dancing, but marching was an honorable activity of
which he approved.

I remember how once when I was sweeping the parlor,
to make the work go faster, I had put a record of one of
Sousa's marches on the little victrola with a morning-
glory horn. I was whirling about the room using the
broom as a dancing partner when Grandfather stormed
inside from the porch, flailing the air with his cane.

"What're you doing in here? There'll be no dancing in
this house while I'm head of it," he scolded.

Up went the broom on my shoulder like a musket and
I paraded noisily back and forth, thumping the broom on
the floor and clicking my bare feet on the rug as hard as
I could.

"I'm not dancing, Granpa, I'm *marching!*"

"Well, see to it that you do march!" he said doubtfully.
I'm sure I never fooled him one bit.

As a child I heard the names of mysterious places
where Grandfather had been and fought—Harpers Ferry,
Antietam, Culpeper, Fredericksburg, Petersburg, Appo-
mattox River, Boston, New Orleans—magic names which
stuck in my memory.

I accepted his military service as the natural consequence of being a Yankee. I did not know then that being
a soldier at all was for him a personal triumph. He was
almost twenty-one and not quite ready for college when
the Civil War began. The clash of arms which disrupted

the nation also threatened the very existence of Ashmum Institute and scattered its student body. Half of the students had to drop out during the first year of the war for lack of tuition and scarcity of scholarships. During the next four years the school came near closing its doors more than once because of threatened raids from Maryland. Conspiracies of official silence would envelop the fate of the Negro race for many weary, uncertain months and higher education for colored men had to await the outcome of the struggle.

By 1861, however, the school had developed a tiny driving force which would emerge as a spearhead of leadership after the war. Six of the young men who pioneered before disunion would be heard from again. Dapper Christian A. Fleetwood, who looked like a dandy and wore heavy sideburns, a long mustache and small tuft of beard, would distinguish himself on the battlefield as sergeant major of the 4th U.S. Colored Troops and become one of the fourteen Negroes in the Civil War to receive the Congressional Medal of Honor. Scholarly Reading B. Johns, who wore glasses and whose heavy curls fell in ringlets about his ears, would press on to a degree from Princeton Theological Seminary and one day would stand before the Connecticut legislature as its chaplain. Brilliant Mahlon Van Horn, from New Jersey, would return after the war to take his degree, go south and be elected to the Mississippi legislature. Later he would serve as United States Consul to the then Danish-held Virgin Islands. William H. Hunter, a preacher from Virginia who had made his way to Pennsylvania to attend the school, would return to his native state after the war and help build the first schools and churches among the freedmen. Peter Plato Hedges would do the same thing in North Carolina. Robert Fitzgerald would work in both states, and the reports sent back from these young men to their school would inspire a steady stream of missionaries to men and women fresh from slavery and eager to learn.

From the very beginning of the war, Robert Fitzgerald was determined to get into the fight. He knew that the blue uniform of the United States was the greatest of all prizes to be won, since those who wore it with honor in defense of their country could no longer be denied the right of citizenship. In this desire my grandfather reflected the universal feeling among the free Negroes of the North. There were no more fervent supporters of the Union cause than they, and they were among the first to rush to the colors when Lincoln called for 75,000 volunteers of three-months' men to subdue the rebellion.

Robert Fitzgerald could not wait to finish school. In company with his brothers, several of his fellow students and some other young men of Hinsonville, he went to the nearest recruiting office to sign up. It was a stinging blow to them when they were told to go home again, the army was not taking colored boys. Never was patriotic enthusiasm crushed by more heavy-handed political expediency. It was the same everywhere in the North. Word had been passed down from Washington not to accept Negroes in the volunteer regiments. Those who had mustered in were quickly mustered out again. The colored people were to have no part in the "white man's war." The free Negro of the North was to be measured by the Negro slave in the South.

Four more slave states left the Union after Lincoln's call for volunteers and he dared not risk the four remaining loyal slave states by putting Negroes into uniform. Most Union officers—some Abolitionists excepted—doubted they'd make good soldiers. Some Yankee troops threatened to lay down their arms and go home and their officers to resign if colored recruits were taken into their ranks. The uniform of the United States might be worn by immigrants just off the boats who could speak no word of English, but not by native-born colored men.

When patriotism collided with prejudice, prejudice was victor. One doughty ex-slave named Nicholas Biddle, who peddled wares around Pottsville, Pennsylvania, had managed to attach himself to a body of troops. Four days after the fall of Fort Sumter he marched with his regiment in full military dress through the streets of Baltimore as the troops changed trains for Washington. Biddle got no farther. White rioters rushed the ranks with clubs and rocks, shouting, "kill the nigger in uniform!" and felled him with a stone that split his head open.

That summer of 1861 was an unbearable one for the Fitzgerald boys. It was cruel for them to have to sit on the side lines while feverish war preparations went on. Banners waved in every township. The villages were suddenly swept clean of their young men. Every able-bodied youth, it seemed, itched to get into the fight to lick the Rebels and teach them a lesson. Meanwhile, invading Union generals were permitting local slaveowners to enter federal lines and reclaim their fugitives while the more realistic Confederates were using their Negro slaves to build the breastworks at Bull Run.

It was galling enough to know that one's country considered one unfit to wear the uniform; it was worse to explain to uninformed local patriots one's presence at home when other young fellows were marching away to the war. There were those intolerable moments when a group of fresh recruits passed the Fitzgerald boys on the road and, not knowing they were colored, yelled out, "Hey, Yank, whyn't you join the colors?" If they gave no answer, the next remark was apt to be, "You must be a damned doughface or a secesh!"

Great-Grandfather Thomas urged his sons to be patient, that the Lord would work it out in His own time and His own way, but patience has never been a virtue of youth. Great-Grandmother Sarah Ann chewed her lips in silence; she could tell them nothing more than to listen to their father. Billy Fitzgerald declared he didn't care much; with a wife and baby to take care of he didn't see any sense in going off to shoot Rebs when there were so many Negro haters right in Pennsylvania; but his brothers knew he was just talking to hear himself talk and to hide his disappointment. Hotheaded eighteen-year-old Richie said he'd break the next man's jaw who asked why he didn't go to fight the secesh, and he got his chance a short while later. Robbie said little; he consoled himself by reading every scrap of war news, following every skirmish and campaign, analyzing every political speech in the newspapers and keeping himself informed.

Then they began to hear of boys they knew joining up with the white regiments and keeping their mouths shut about their race. Sixteen-year-old Edwin Belcher from Philadelphia slipped off and joined the 73rd Pennsylvania Volunteers that August. He was to serve with his regiment throughout the war, rising from private to captain and becoming a hero in the battle of Lookout Mountain, Tennessee, in October, 1863. When he was discharged with honor nobody in his company was the wiser.

Well, that was one way of getting around all the humbug about not letting colored men fight as soldiers. Pennsylvania, with her twenty thousand mulattoes, was a natural breeding ground for this sort of thing. Before the war was many weeks old thousands of mixed bloods were entering white regiments. Some never recrossed the line

and others were not known in the official records as Negroes until many years later when they applied for their
pensions. An incredible number of patriotic "Indians,"
curly-haired "Mexicans," swarthy "Italians" and dingy
"Irish" began showing up at the recruiting places. Local
officers weren't too particular how they filled their quotas
as long as no fuss was made, and a man who could pass for
anything but colored was readily accepted.

The Fitzgerald boys considered this course, but it
would have been an act of disloyalty to their father,
whom they revered, to have gone off somewhere and
joined up as white men. He'd always taught them,
"Never be ashamed of what you are. Just be the best you
can be and show what colored men can do when they
have the chance." To join a white regiment would be
taking all the credit from the black side of the ledger
which needed desperately to prove that colored men were
brave and giving it to the white side which needed no
boosts. One's courage only built the white race higher
without proving a thing about the colored man.

A Negro who "passed" was like a spy, watchful of every
move, fearful of being exposed by a chance meeting with
an old acquaintance. If his fellows found out about his
race, they were likely to drum him out of camp as they
would a traitor or thief. Ashamed of the low jokes they'd
told about "niggers," "darkies" and "baboons" in his
presence—jeers they wouldn't dare repeat before any self-
respecting colored man—they'd feel betrayed and in their
guilt they'd turn upon him as the coward and sneak. Such
a man nearly always found himself enduring the coarse
jokes and insults in silence or joining in the vulgar laughter to show that he was part of the crowd. Pretty soon he
would grow to hate himself, for having denied part of
himself he would not be able to accept the other part and
wound up hating both.

It would take more than official rebuffs to keep a Fitzgerald out of the fight altogether. That summer a big
Union supply depot opened in Perryville, Maryland, on
the banks of the Susquehanna River, to receive mules
and animals for the Bull Run campaign and to move
supplies southward for the troops. To transport its supplies from the North to the southern fighting fronts, the
Union needed a large force of teamsters, wagon masters,
mule drivers and hostlers for the long wagon trains. It
also needed wheelwrights and blacksmiths, road and
bridge builders. The Quartermasters of the Civil War
had no troops; they hired civilians to perform these tasks.
They took on men as they needed them and let them go
again when a big campaign was over. Laborers' pay was
$20 a month; a teamster got $25, a wagonmaster $35, and
the pay increased with the various skills.

Word passed around that the Quartermaster's Department had a recruiting office at Fifth and Walnut streets
in Philadelphia and was hiring every able-bodied man it
could find who was not under arms. The Fitzgerald boys
and other young colored men from Chester County answered the call. They could handle horses and mules, the
pay was good and they'd be in the war at last. Robert
Fitzgerald packed his books and put them away, stuffed
a small Bible and a tiny sketchbook in his shirt pocket
and followed his brothers to Philadelphia, where they
all signed up and were sent down to Perryville along with
some of their Burton and Valentine cousins.

Great-Grandfather Thomas joined his sons and hired
out as teamster and assistant wagonmaster for several
months that winter but returned to his crops when spring
planting time came around. In early 1862, the Fitzgerald
brothers were transferred to the Washington supply base
and scattered throughout Virginia as the Peninsular
Campaign got under way. Richard spent most of that year

driving mules around Harrison's Landing and Fortress Monroe, swearing and fuming each time he lost a bucket from underneath his wagon and had two dollars docked from his pay. Billy wound up driving a one-horse cart on detail at Acquia Creek, while Robbie landed in a construction corps with Banks' army building corduroy roads and pontoon bridges.

For one of delicate health he chalked up an amazing record during the next two years. When he was not chopping down trees and building roads and bridges, he was driving a team in the wagon train or filling in as a company cook in a regiment. He proved a reliable worker and sometimes he was detached from his outfit and sent hurriedly from place to place delivering cavalry horses. He said these lonely pilgrimages were the most terrifying because death to him was better than being captured by the Rebels. He was at Harpers Ferry building pontoon bridges in late summer, 1862, and got out just before the federal garrison with its eleven thousand men and large stores of equipment fell to Stonewall Jackson. He delivered horses to Antietam, to Culpeper and to Warrenton, Virginia. He hauled pontoons from Acquia Creek and help to lay them across the Rappahannock River under murderous Rebel fire just before the Union troops gallantly but vainly stormed the heights of Fredericksburg.

It was a mean life which offered neither the prestige of a uniform nor the protection of a musket. Of all the branches of the service, the Quartermasters' men were the least trained, least educated, least organized, least protected in battle and most maligned of the Civil War. The teamster and laborer crews were the motliest assortment of men ever collected for a mass operation. The great war machine had gathered up "contrabands"—ragged slaves who escaped to the Union lines and offered themselves as cooks, scouts, guides or pick-and-shovel men. It recruited tatterdemalions and drunks; desperadoes and thieves; stragglers and bummers who sought refuge in the rear; hard-bitten farmers who fought the war between crops; seedy, decrepit old fellows who had been rejected for service under arms; Indians and immigrants, "free issues" and "we sorts"; mysterious men who came out of the shadows lured by the Quartermasters' pay and vanished again when the war ended; and eager young colored men from the northern and middle states patiently waiting to prove themselves.

They were there because the Quartermasters asked no questions about background or race and wanted only to get the job done. The Quartermasters were having a hard time at that and took what they could get. They had no regulation clothing or equipment for their men; their ragamuffin corps looked like an army of scarecrows. They wore what they could buy, beg, borrow or steal, odds and ends which gave them a dilapidated appearance but usually some cast-off insignia which stamped them unmistakably as Union men.

There was nothing to make a man stick to this disreputable-looking army except the pay, sheer love of excitement, or an idealism stronger than the abuse heaped upon its members. Yet Grandfather Fitzgerald and many others like him stuck, endured the jeers and humiliations, the curses and abominations which offended his pride and aroused his resentment. He drove his body to limits his mother would not have believed possible, clamped restraints upon his indignation, ignored the taunts and kept going. When there was a halt or rest, he'd take out his Bible and read a chapter or sketch in his notebook a bridge, a river bank or a general riding past. Day by day through menial tasks he was earning his citizenship.

The most that could be said for his ignominious drudg-

ery was that he was in the thick of things, sharing the
dangers and hardships with the rest. The teamster and
laborer crews were the fighting man's lifeline. He relied
upon the Quartermasters' civilian army to set up supply
bases, field hospitals and army headquarters; to provide
transportation for the wounded and prisoners of war; re-
placements of horses and mules lost in battle; to lay telegraph lines and railroad tracks; to keep a continuous flow
of food, guns, ammunition, medical equipment; forage
for animals and luggage for field and staff officers moving
from Washington down to men on the battlefronts.

Wherever the armies went, the wagon trains followed
or sometimes even plowed ahead to build and stock supply bases, drop off crews to lay down plank roads or corduroy roads for the troops or throw up bridges over rivers
and creeks. Day and night Washington residents heard
the unbroken thunder of heavy wheels and hoofs on the
cobblestone streets as the wagon trains rumbled southward across Long Bridge or straggled back again bringing
wounded and dying men from the front lines. When a
whole army was on the march, at its rear wound the
long, snaking line of canvas-topped wagons, five hundred
strong and miles in length, weaving and bobbing up and
down the ridges like a giant white caterpillar, throwing
up great columns of dust over the countryside.

Grandfather usually drove a four-horse or six-mule
team but there was every conceivable type of team in the
line when it started out—regimental wagons carrying
medical supplies, regimental papers, luggage, small-arms
ammunition and field artillery; two-horse ambulances;
forage wagons bulging with hay for the animals; kitchen
wagons loaded with bags of coffee, barrels of beef and
pork, boxes of bread, kettles, pots and pans, and company cooks armed with nothing more defensive than a

butcher's knife or iron skillet. The endless white line was broken here and there by the black-topped sutlers' carts which followed the armies and peddled tobacco, newspapers, sweetmeats and other wares to the soldiers. Up and down the line rode wagon masters, urging teams forward to fill long gaps, untangling snarls and pulling crippled wagons out of the way. The wagon masters were sometimes accompanied by volunteer corps and a guard usually escorted the trains behind and in front to protect them from Rebel skirmishers' fire.

Moving men under orders on a forced march with rifles and bayonets for protection was one thing; moving untrained civilian drivers and mules over the dust-choked or mud-clogged roads in all kinds of weather was another. Wagons broke down or sank to their axles in mire. Men beat and cursed their mules and the mules balked. Delay upon delay piled up the teams, jammed the roads, snarled the traffic and held up vital supplies. Crossing small streams, drivers often ignored the water buckets under their wagons and let their animals stop midstream to drink, obstructing passage and causing more delays. Dust strangled and blinded the men; animals dropped dead from exhaustion and bad treatment; supply lines crawled, stopped, crawled again; battles were lost because ammunition never arrived in time; wounded men died because they did not reach hospitals quickly enough. Trains could seldom move more than fourteen to seventeen miles a day in the best of summer weather; in winter, a day's march slowed down to twelve miles.

Mix-ups along the road were bad enough, but encampments were sheer bedlam. When marching troops halted and bivouacked for the night, the men usually fell out and camped off the roadside in the nearest grove or clearing. Miles behind, their regimental wagons seldom caught up with them until several hours later. Teams could not jump ditches or maneuver about in gulches as could men on foot, and drivers had to jog along the road looking for a convenient turnoff, jamming traffic again and milling about in confusion until regimental guides rescued them and led them to their regiments. Often it was nearly midnight when kitchen teams showed up, and the fighting men who had run out of rations and couldn't borrow any had to go to bed without supper, roundly cursing the drivers in particular and the entire Quartermasters' Corps in general. Before dawn the unwieldy, fragmentized caterpillar which had scattered into hundreds of pieces during the night had to reassemble, but it was hours before the ungainly caravan was bobbing down the road again. Miles behind its marching men it was often cut off by flank movements of the enemy and left to disintegrate in pandemonium.

Sometimes the teams had hardly unhitched for the night when orders arrived that a segment of the train be detached and follow a body of troops elsewhere. Drivers set out, traveling without lights, their sole guide a dingy white pocket handkerchief pinned to the back of the wagon master at the head of the line. They drove as hard and fast as they could over roads that oozed black mud from steady rains and the churnings of thousands of horses and men, often without guard and in plain sight of Rebel campfires, raked by skirmishers' fire.

Soldiers in the front columns usually sensed the pull and tug of the battle lines and were often more aware of impending victory or defeat than their generals. Not so with the unarmed teamsters in the rear, who lived in a fog of rumors and tangled movements. They were the last to know what was going on and the first to be slaughtered when lines caved in suddenly and there was a bloody rout. Chaos prevailed when a fighting line collapsed and men streamed to the rear. Trains lost their wagon masters and regiments, drivers went mad with fear, cut loose their animals and fled into the woods, or were shot and sabered by Confederate cavalrymen. Driverless horses and mules stampeded, wagons overturned scattering supplies and equipment in all directions and barring roads to retreat. When the panic subsided and some semblance of order was restored, the laborers' corps were sent out on the battlefields to bring in the wounded, bury corpses and rescue what equipment they could.

Throughout the war, enlisted men swore at the teamsters and the teamsters swore at their animals and the holy crusade to save the Union mired in muck and blood and the fields of Virginia stank with unburied corpses. The Quartermasters appealed for uniforms, guns and training for their men but their pleas were ignored. It was not the glory in battle Robert Fitzgerald dreamed of, and yet, however much the boys in blue sneered at the teamsters and contrabands, the Quartermasters' reports gave mounting evidence of the thankless toil of these men in the long nightmare of advances and retreats.

The black men were good workers, steady under fire, eager to follow orders and help the Union; they bore more fatigue and exposure than many of the white soldiers and laborers, and their assistance was of immense value to the Union army. In fact, at the end of 1862, Quartermaster-General M. C. Meigs reported that the large numbers of Negroes employed for the necessary labor of the army posts had freed the white soldier to perform his purely military duties, "and enabled him to preserve his health and acquire that proficiency in drill and the use of arms which has made the troops in the Department of the South so efficient in every field."

Fine, thought young men like Robert Fitzgerald, but not enough. If they must bear the risks of war, let them at least have recognition as soldiers and the dignity of uniforms. What Grandfather did not realize then was that he and his father, brothers, cousins and thousands of other colored men were building a record which slowly wore down the resistance to the idea of Negroes in Yankee uniforms.

4

"Men of Color, To Arms"
by Frederick Douglass
(1817–1895)

It was military necessity that finally forced the North to arm the Negroes. On July 17, 1862, Congress passed two acts providing for the enlistment of Negroes as soldiers. The first was the Confiscation Act, which allowed the President "to employ as many persons of African descent as he may deem necessary and proper for the suppression of this rebellion." The second was a Militia Act repealing the provisions of the 1792 law barring colored men and authorizing the employment of free Negroes and freedmen as soldiers.

Frederick Douglass was one of the most persistent advocates for the arming of Negroes. He felt that if the black man could prove his equality on the battlefront, he would no longer be a second-class citizen. The following appeal was printed as a broadside on March 2, 1863, in Rochester, New York.

When first the rebel cannon shattered the walls of Sumter and drove away its starving garrison, I predicted that the war then and there inaugurated would not be fought out entirely by white men. Every month's experience during these dreary years has confirmed that opinion. A war un-

dertaken and brazenly carried on for the perpetual en-
slavement of colored men, calls logically and loudly for
colored men to help suppress it. Only a moderate share
of sagacity was needed to see that the arm of the slave
was the best defense against the arm of the slaveholder.
Hence, with every reverse to the national arms, with
every exulting shout of victory raised by the slaveholding
rebels, I have implored the imperiled nation to unchain
against her foes her powerful black hand. Slowly and reluctantly that appeal is beginning to be heeded. Stop not
now to complain that it was not heeded sooner. That it
should not may or may not have been best. This is not
the time to discuss that question. Leave it to the future.
When the war is over, the country saved, peace established and the black man's rights are secured, as they will
be, history with an impartial hand will dispose of that
and sundry other questions. Action! action! not criticism,
is the plain duty of this hour. Words are now useful only
as they stimulate to blows. The office of speech now is
only to point out when, where, and how to strike to the
best advantage. There is no time to delay. The tide is at
its flood that leads on to fortune. From East to West, from
North to South, the sky is written all over, 'NOW OR
NEVER.' Liberty won by white men would lose half its
luster. 'Who would be free themselves must strike the
blow.' 'Better even die free, than to live slaves.' This is
the sentiment of every brave colored man amongst us.
There are weak and cowardly men in all nations. We
have them amongst us. They tell you this is the 'white
man's war'; that you 'will be no better off after than
before the war'; that the getting of you into the Army is
to 'sacrifice you on the first opportunity.' Believe them
not; cowards themselves, they do not wish to have their
cowardice shamed by your brave example. Leave them

to their timidity, or to whatever motive may hold them back. I have not thought lightly of the words I am now addressing you. The counsel I give comes of close observation of the great struggle now in progress, and of the deep conviction that this is your hour and mine. In good earnest, then, and after the best deliberation, I now, for the first time during this war, feel at liberty to call and counsel you to arms. By every consideration which binds you to your enslaved fellow-countrymen and to the peace and welfare of your country; by every aspiration which you cherish for the freedom and equality of yourselves and your children; by all the ties of blood and identity which make us one with the brave black men now fighting our battles in Louisiana and in South Carolina, I urge you to fly to arms, and smite with death the power that would bury the Government and your liberty in the same hopeless grave. I wish I could tell you that the State of New York calls you to this high honor. For the moment her constituted authorities are silent on the subject. They will speak by and by, and doubtless on the right side; but we are not compelled to wait for her. We can get at the throat of treason and slavery through the State of Massachusetts. She was first in the War of Independence; first to break the chains of her slaves; first to make the black man equal before the law; first to admit colored children to her common schools, and she was first to answer with her blood the alarm-cry of the nation, when its capital was menaced by rebels. You know her patriotic governor, and you know Charles Sumner. I need not add more.

Massachusetts now welcomes you to arms as soldiers. She has but a small colored population from which to recruit. She has full leave of the general government to send one regiment to the war, and she has undertaken to do it. Go quickly and help fill up the first colored regiment from the North. I am authorized to assure you that you will receive the same wages, the same rations, the same equipments, the same protection, the same treatment, and the same bounty, secured to white soldiers. You will be led by able and skillful officers, men who will take especial pride in your efficiency and success. They will be quick to accord to you all the honor you shall merit by your valor, and to see that your rights and feelings are respected by other soldiers. I have assured myself on these points, and can speak with authority. More than twenty years of unswerving devotion to our common cause may give me some humble claim to be trusted at this momentous crisis. I will not argue. To do so implies hesitation and doubt, and you do not hesitate. You do not doubt. The day dawns; the morning star is bright upon the horizon! The iron gate of our prison stands half open. One gallant rush from the North will fling it wide open, while four millions of our brothers and sisters shall march out into liberty. The chance is now given you to end in a day the bondage of centuries, and to rise in one bound from social degradation to the place of common equality with all other varieties of men. Remember Denmark Vesey [sic] of Charleston; remember Nathaniel Turner of South Hampton; remember Shields Green and Copeland, who followed noble John Brown, and fell as glorious martyrs for the cause of the slave. Remember that in a contest with oppression, the Almighty has no attribute which can take sides with oppressors. The case is before you. This is our golden opportunity. Let us accept it, and forever wipe out the dark reproaches unsparingly hurled against us by our enemies. Let us win for ourselves the gratitude of our country, and the best blessings of our posterity through all time. The nucleus of this first regiment is now at Readville, a short distance from Boston. I will undertake to forward to Boston all persons adjudged fit to be mustered into the regiment, who shall apply to me at any time within the next two weeks.

5

FROM

Army Life in a Black Regiment

by Thomas Wentworth Higginson
(1823–1911)

*The man chosen to lead the first regiment of black sol-
diers was Thomas Wentworth Higginson, a Boston aristo-
crat, a Unitarian minister, a writer and lecturer, and a
militant abolitionist. He was a captain in the Fifty-first
Massachusetts Militia when he received the letter which
offered him the command, with the rank of colonel, of
the newly formed First South Carolina Volunteers, encamped near Beaufort, South Carolina.*

*Most northern whites believed that black men, espe-
cially ex-slaves, were too cowardly and servile to be good
soldiers. It was Higginson's job to disprove this opinion,
and it never occurred to him for a minute that he would
fail. He believed in his men, and they, in turn, did not
fail that trust. Higginson's diary, portions of which are
reprinted here, is a dramatic record of the black soldier's
participation in the Civil War.*

November 27, 1862.

Thanksgiving-Day; it is the first moment I have had
for writing during these three days, which have installed
me into a new mode of life so thoroughly that they seem
three years. Scarcely pausing in New York or in Beaufort,

there seems to have been for me but one step from the camp of a Massachusetts regiment to this, and that step over leagues of waves.

It is a holiday wherever General Saxton's proclamation reaches. The chilly sunshine and the pale blue river seems like New England, but those alone. The air is full of noisy drumming, and of gunshots; for the prize-shooting is our great celebration of the day, and the drumming is chronic. My young barbarians are all at play. I look out from the broken windows of this forlorn plantation-house, through avenues of great live-oaks, with their hard, shining leaves, and their branches hung with a universal drapery of soft, long moss, like fringe-trees struck with grayness. Below, the sandy soil, scantily covered with coarse grass, bristles with sharp palmettoes and aloes; all the vegetation is stiff, shining, semi-tropical, with nothing soft or delicate in its texture. Numerous plantation-buildings totter around, all slovenly and unattractive, while the interspaces are filled with all manner of wreck and refuse, pigs, fowls, dogs, and omnipresent Ethiopian infancy. All this is the universal Southern panorama; but five minutes' walk beyond the hovels and the live-oaks will bring one to something so un-Southern that the whole Southern coast at this moment trembles at the suggestion of such a thing,—the camp of a regiment of freed slaves.

One adapts one's self so readily to new surroundings that already the full zest of the novelty seems passing away from my perceptions, and I write these lines in an eager effort to retain all I can. Already I am growing used to the experience, at first so novel, of living among five hundred men, and scarce a white face to be seen,—of seeing them go through all their daily processes, eating, frolicking, talking, just as if they were white. Each day at dress-parade I stand with the customary folding of the arms before a regimental line of countenances so black that I can hardly tell whether the men stand steadily or not; black is every hand which moves in ready cadence as I vociferate, "Battalion! Shoulder arms!" nor is it till the line of white officers moves forward, as parade is dismissed, that I am reminded that my own face is not the color of coal.

The first few days on duty with a new regiment must be devoted almost wholly to tightening reins; in this process one deals chiefly with the officers, and I have as yet had but little personal intercourse with the men. They concern me chiefly in bulk, as so many consumers of rations, wearers of uniforms, bearers of muskets. But as the machine comes into shape, I am beginning to decipher the individual parts. At first, of course, they all looked just alike; the variety comes afterwards, and they are just as distinguishable, the officers say, as so many whites. Most of them are wholly raw, but there are many who have already been for months in camp in the abortive "Hunter Regiment," yet in that loose kind of way which, like average militia training, is a doubtful advantage. I notice that some companies, too, look darker than others, though all are purer African than I expected. This is said to be partly a geographical difference between the South Carolina and Florida men. When the Rebels evacuated this region they probably took with them the house-servants, including most of the mixed blood, so that the residuum seems very black. But the men brought from Fernandina the other day average lighter in complexion, and look more intelligent, and they certainly take wonderfully to the drill.

It needs but a few days to show the absurdity of distrusting the military availability of these people. They have quite as much average comprehension as whites of the need of the thing, as much courage (I doubt not), as much previous knowledge of the gun, and, above all, a readiness of ear and of limitation, which, for purposes of drill, counterbalances any defect of mental training. To learn the drill, one does not want a set of college professors; one wants a squad of eager, active, pliant schoolboys; and the more childlike these pupils are the better. There is no trouble about the drill; they will surpass whites in that. As to camp-life, they have little to sacrifice; they are better fed, housed, and clothed than ever in their lives before, and they appear to have few inconvenient vices. They are simple, docile, and affectionate almost to the point of absurdity. The same men who stood fire in open field with perfect coolness, on the late expedition, have come to me blubbering in the most irresistibly ludicrous manner on being transferred from one company in the regiment to another.

In noticing the squad-drills I perceive that the men learn less laboriously than whites that "double, double, toil and trouble," which is the elementary vexation of the drill-master,—that they more rarely mistake their left for their right,—and are more grave and sedate while under instruction. The extremes of jollity and sobriety, being greater with them, are less liable to be intermingled; these companies can be driven with a looser rein than my former one, for they restrain themselves; but the moment they are dismissed from drill every tongue is relaxed and every ivory tooth visible. This morning I wandered about where the different companies were target-shooting, and their glee was contagious. Such exulting shouts of "ki! ole man," when some steady old turkey-shooter brought his gun down for an instant's aim, and then unerringly hit the mark; and then, when some unwary youth fired his piece into the ground at half-cock such guffawing and delight, rolling over and over on the grass, such dances of ecstasy, as made the "Ethiopian minstrelsy" of the stage appear a feeble imitation.

Evening.—Better still was a scene on which I stumbled to-night. Strolling in the cool moonlight, I was attracted by a brilliant light beneath the trees, and cautiously approached it. A circle of thirty or forty soldiers sat around a roaring fire, while one old uncle, Cato by name, was narrating an interminable tale, to the insatiable delight of his audience. I came up into the dusky background, perceived only by a few, and he still continued. It was a narrative, dramatized to the last degree, of his adventures in escaping from his master to the Union vessels; and even I, who have heard the stories of Harriet Tubman, and such wondeful slave-comedians, never witnessed such a piece of acting. When I came upon the scene he had just come unexpectedly upon a plantation-house, and, putting a bold face upon it, had walked up to the door.

"Den I go up to de white man, berry humble, and say, would he please gib ole man a mouthful for eat?

"He say he must hab de valeration ob half a dollar.

"Den I look berry sorry, and turn for go away.

"Den he say I might gib him dat hatchet I had.

"Den I say" (this in a tragic vein) "dat I must hab dat hatchet for defend myself *from de dogs!*"

[Immense applause, and one appreciating auditor says, chuckling, "Dat was your *arms,* ole man," which brings down the house again.]

"Den he say de Yankee pickets was near by, and I must be very keerful.

"Den I say, 'Good Lord, Mas'r, am dey?' "

Words cannot express the complete dissimulation with which these accents of terror were uttered,—this being precisely the piece of information he wished to obtain.

Then he narrated his devices to get into the house at night and obtain some food,—how a dog flew at him,—how he scrambled under a hedge and over a high fence, etc.,—all in a style of which Gough alone among the orators can give the faintest impression, so thoroughly dramatized was every syllable.

Then he described his reaching the river-side at last, and trying to decide whether certain vessels held friends or foes.

"Den I see guns on board, and sure sartin he Union boat, and I pop my head up. Den I been-a-tink [think] Seceshkey hab guns too, and my head go down again. Den I hide in de bush till morning. Den I open my bundle, and take ole white shirt and tie him on ole pole and wave him, and ebry time de wind blow, I been-a-tremble, and drap down in de bushes,"—because, being between two fires, he doubted whether friend or foe would see his signal first. And so on, with a succession of tricks beyond Molière, of acts of caution, foresight, patient cunning, which were listened to with infinite gusto and perfect comprehension by every listener.

And all this to a bivouac of negro soldiers, with the brilliant fire lighting up their red trousers and gleaming from their shining black faces,—eyes and teeth all white with tumultuous glee. Overhead, the mighty limbs of a great live-oak, with the weird moss swaying in the smoke, and the high moon gleaming faintly through.

Yet to-morrow strangers will remark on the hopeless, impenetrable stupidity in the daylight faces of many of these very men, the solid mask under which Nature has concealed all this wealth of mother-wit. This very comedian is one to whom one might point, as he hoed lazily in a cotton-field, as a being the light of whose brain had utterly gone out; and this scene seems like coming by night upon some conclave of black beetles, and finding them engaged, with green-room and foot-lights, in enacting "Poor Pillicoddy." This is their university; every young Sambo before me, as he turned over the sweet potatoes and peanuts which were roasting in the ashes, listened with reverence to the wiles of the ancient Ulysses, and meditated the same. It is Nature's compensation; oppression simply crushes the upper faculties of the head, and crowds everything into the perceptive organs. Cato, thou reasonest well! When I get into any serious scrape, in an enemy's country, may I be lucky enough to have you at my elbow, to pull me out of it!

The men seem to have enjoyed the novel event of Thanksgiving Day; they have had company and regimental prize-shootings, a minimum of speeches and a maximum of dinner. Bill of fare: two beef-cattle and a thousand oranges. The oranges cost a cent apiece, and the cattle were Secesh, bestowed by General Saxby, as they all call him.

January 1, 1863 (evening).

A happy New Year to civilized people,—mere white folks. Our festival has come and gone, with perfect success, and our good General has been altogether satisfied. Last night the great fires were kept smouldering in the pit, and the beeves were cooked more or less, chiefly more,—during which time they had to be carefully watched, and the great spits turned by main force. Happy were the merry fellows who were permitted to sit up all night, and watch the glimmering flames that threw a thousand fantastic shadows among the great gnarled oaks. And such a chattering as I was sure to hear whenever I awoke that night!

My first greeting to-day was from one of the most stylish sergeants, who approached me with the following little speech, evidently the result of some elaboration:—

"I tink myself happy, dis New Year's Day, for salute my own Cunnel. Dis day las' year I was servant to a Cunnel ob Secesh; but now I hab de privilege for salute my own Cunnel."

That officer, with the utmost sincerity, reciprocated the sentiment.

About ten o'clock the people began to collect by land, and also by water,—in steamers sent by General Saxton for the purpose; and from that time all the avenues of approach were thronged. The multitude were chiefly colored women, with gay handkerchiefs on their heads, and a sprinkling of men, with that peculiarly respectable look which these people always have on Sundays and holidays. There were many white visitors also,—ladies on horseback and in carriages, superintendents and teachers, officers, and cavalry-men. Our companies were marched to the neighborhood of the platform, and allowed to sit or stand, as at the Sunday services; the platform was occupied by ladies and dignitaries, and by the band of the Eighth Maine, which kindly volunteered for the occasion; the colored people filled up all the vacant openings in the beautiful grove around, and there was a cordon of mounted visitors beyond. Above, the great live-oak branches and their trailing moss; beyond the people, a glimpse of the blue river.

The services began at half past eleven o'clock, with prayer by our chaplain, Mr. Fowler, who is always, on such occasions, simple, reverential, and impressive. Then the President's Proclamation was read by Dr. W. H. Brisbane, a thing infinitely appropriate, a South Carolinian addressing South Carolinians; for he was reared among these very islands, and here long since emancipated his own slaves. Then the colors were presented to us by the

Rev. Mr. French, a chaplain who brought them from the donors in New York. All this was according to the programme. Then followed an incident so simple, so touching, so utterly unexpected and startling, that I can scarcely believe it on recalling, though it gave the keynote to the whole day. The very moment the speaker had ceased, and just as I took and waved the flag, which now for the first time meant anything to these poor people, there suddenly arose, close beside the platform, a strong male voice (but rather cracked and elderly), into which two women's voices instantly blended, singing, as if by an impulse that could no more be repressed than the morning note of the song-sparrow.—

"My Country, 'tis of thee,
Sweet land of liberty,
Of thee I sing!"

People looked at each other, and then at us on the platform, to see whence came this interruption, not set down in the bills. Firmly and irrepressibly the quavering voices sang on, verse after verse; others of the colored people joined in; some whites on the platform began, but I motioned them to silence. I never saw anything so electric; it made all other words cheap; it seemed the choked voice of a race at last unloosed. Nothing could be more wonderfully unconscious; art could not have dreamed of a tribute to the day of jubilee that should be so affecting; history will not believe it; and when I came to speak of it, after it was ended, tears were everywhere. If you could have heard how quaint and innocent it was! Old Tiff and his children might have sung it; and close before me was a little slave-boy, almost white, who seemed to belong to the party, and even he must join in. Just think of it!—the first day they had ever had a country, the first flag they had ever seen which promised anything to their people, and here, while mere spectators stood in silence, waiting for my stupid words, these simple souls burst out in their lay, as if they were by their own hearths at home! When they stopped, there was nothing to do for it but to speak, and I went on; but the life of the whole day was in those unknown people's song.

Receiving the flags, I gave them into the hands of two fine-looking men, jet black, as color-guard and they also spoke, and very effectively,—Sergeant Prince Rivers and Corporal Robert Sutton. The regiment sang "Marching Along," and then General Saxton spoke, in his own simple, manly way, and Mrs. Francis D. Gage spoke very sensibly to the women, and Judge Stickney, from Florida, added something; then some gentleman sang an ode, and the regiment the John Brown song, and then they went to their beef and molasses. Everything was very orderly, and they seemed to have a very gay time. Most of the visitors had far to go, and so dispersed before dress-parade, though the band stayed to enliven it. In the evening we had letters from home, and General Saxton had a reception at his house, from which I excused myself; and so ended one of the most enthusiastic and happy gatherings I ever knew. The day was perfect, and there was nothing but success.

I forgot to say, that, in the midst of the services, it was announced that General Fremont was appointed Commander-in-Chief,—an announcement which was received with immense cheering, as would have been almost anything else, I verily believe, at that moment of high tide. It was shouted across by the pickets above,—a way in which we often receive news, but not always trustworthy.

It was after midnight when we set off upon our excursion. I had about a hundred men, marching by the flank, with a small advanced guard, and also a few flankers, where the ground permitted. I put my Florida company at the head of the column, and had by my side Captain Metcalf, an excellent officer, and Sergeant McIntyre, his first sergeant. We plunged presently in pine woods, whose resinous smell I can still remember. Corporal Sutton marched near me, with his captured negro guide, whose first fear and sullenness had yielded to the magic news of the President's [Emancipation] Proclamation, then just issued, of which Governor Andrew had sent me a large printed supply;—we seldom found men who could read it, but they all seemed to feel more secure when they held it in their hands. We marched on through the woods, with no sound but the peeping of the frogs in a neighboring marsh, and the occasional yelping of a dog, as we passed the hut of some "cracker." This yelping always made Corporal Sutton uneasy; dogs are the detective officers of Slavery's police.

We had halted once or twice to close up the ranks, and had marched some two miles, seeing and hearing nothing more. I had got all I could out of our new guide, and was striding on, rapt in pleasing contemplation. All had gone so smoothly that I had merely to fancy the rest as being equally smooth. Already I fancied our little detachment bursting out of the woods, in swift surprise, upon the Rebel quarters,—already the opposing commander, after hastily firing a charge or two from his revolver (of course above my head), had yielded at discretion, and was gracefully tendering, in a stage attitude, his unavailing sword, —when suddenly—

There was a trampling of feet among the advanced guard as they came confusedly to a halt, and almost at the same instant a more ominous sound, as of galloping horses in the path before us. The moonlight outside the woods gave that dimness of atmosphere within which is more bewildering than darkness, because the eyes cannot adapt themselves to it so well. Yet I fancied, and others aver, that they saw the leader of an approaching party mounted on a white horse and reining up in the pathway; others, again, declare that he drew a pistol from the holster and took aim; others heard the words, "Charge in upon them! Surround them!" But all this was confused by the opening rifle-shots of our advanced guard, and, as clear observation was impossible, I made the men fix their bayonets and kneel in the cover on each side the pathway, and I saw with delight the brave fellows, with Sergeant McIntyre at their head, settling down in the grass as coolly and warily as if wild turkeys were the only game. Perhaps at the first shot a man fell at my elbow. I felt it no more than if a tree had fallen,—I was so busy watching my own men and the enemy, and planning what to do next. Some of our soldiers, misunderstanding the order, "Fix bayonets," were actually *charging* with them, dashing off into the dim woods, with nothing to charge at but the vanishing tail of an imaginary horse,— for we could really see nothing. This zeal I noted with pleasure, and also with anxiety, as our greatest danger was from confusion and scattering; and for infantry to pursue cavalry would be a novel enterprise. Captain Metcalf stood by me well in keeping the men steady, as did Assistant Surgeon Minor, and Lieutenant, now Captain, Jackson. How the men in the rear were behaving I could not tell,—not so coolly, I afterwards found, because they were more entirely bewildered, supposing, until the shots came, that the column had simply halted for a moment's rest, as had been done once or twice before. They did not know who or where their assailants might be, and the fall of the man beside me created a hasty rumor that I was killed, so that it was on the whole an alarming experience for them. They kept together very tolerably, however, while our assailants, dividing, rode along each side through the open pine-barren, firing into our ranks, but mostly over the heads of the men. My soldiers in turn fired rapidly,—too rapidly, being yet beginners,—and it was evident that, dim as it was, both sides had opportunity to do some execution.

I could hardly tell whether the fight had lasted ten minutes or an hour, when, as the enemy's fire had evidently ceased or slackened, I gave the order to cease firing. But it was very difficult at first to make them desist: the taste of gunpowder was too intoxicating. One of them was heard to muttter, indignantly, "Why de Cunnel order *Cease firing*, when de Secesh blazin' away at de rate ob ten dollar a day?" Every incidental occurrence seemed somehow to engrace itself upon my perceptions, without interrupting the main course of thought. Thus I know, that, in one of the pauses of the affair, there came wailing through the woods a cracked female voice, as if calling back some stray husband who had run out to join the affray, "John, John, are you going to leave me, John? Are you going to let me and the children be killed, John?" I suppose the poor thing's fears of gunpowder were very genuine; but it was such a wailing squeak, and so infinitely ludicrous, and John was probably esconced so very safely in some hollow tree, that I could see some of the men showing all their white teeth in the very midst of the fight. But soon this sound, with all others, had ceased, and left us in peaceful possession of the field.

I have made the more of this little affair because it was the first stand-up fight in which my men had been engaged, though they had been under fire, in an irregular way, in their small early expeditions. To me personally the event was of the greatest value; it had given us all an opportunity to test each other, and our abstract surmises were changed into positive knowledge. Hereafter it was of small importance what nonsense might be talked or written about colored troops; as long as mine did not flinch, it made no difference to me. My brave young officers, themselves mostly new to danger, viewed the matter much as I did; and yet we were under bonds of life and death to form a correct opinion, which was more than could be said of the Northern editors, and our verdict was proportionately of greater value.

I was convinced from appearances that we had been victorious, so far, though I could not suppose that this would be the last of it. We knew neither the numbers of the enemy, nor their plans, nor their present condition: whether they had surprised us or whether we had surprised them was all a mystery. Corporal Sutton was urgent to go on and complete the enterprise. All my impulses said the same thing; but then I had the most explicit injunctions from General Saxton to risk as little as possible in this enterprise, because of the fatal effect on public sentiment of even an honorable defeat. We had now an honorable victory, so far as it went; the officers and men around me were in good spirits, but the rest of the column might be nervous; and it seemed so important to make the first fight an entire success, that I thought it wiser to let well alone; nor have I ever changed this opinion. For one's self, Montrose's verse may be well applied, "To win or lose it all." But one has no right to deal thus lightly with the fortunes of a race, and that was the weight which I always felt as resting in our action. If my raw infantry force had stood unflinchingly a night-surprise from "de hoss cavalry," as they reverentially termed them, I felt that a good beginning had been made. All hope of surprising the enemy's camp was not at an end; I was willing and ready to fight the cavalry over again, but it seemed wiser that we, not they, should select the ground.

Attending to the wounded, therefore, and making as we best could stretchers for those who were to be carried, including the remains of the man killed at the first discharge (Private William Parsons of Company G), and others who seemed at the point of death, we marched through the woods to the landing,—expecting at every moment to be involved in another fight. This not occurring, I was more than ever satisfied that we had won a victory; for it was obvious that a mounted force would not allow a detachment of infantry to march two miles through open woods by night without renewing the fight, unless they themselves had suffered a good deal. On arrival at the landing, seeing that there was to be no immediate affray, I sent most of the men on board, and called for volunteers to remain on shore with me and hold the plantation-house till morning. They eagerly offered; and I was glad to see them, when posted as sentinels by Lieutenants Hyde and Jackson, who stayed with me, pace their beats as steadily and challenge as coolly as veterans, though of course there was some powder wasted on imaginary foes. Greatly to my surprise, however, we had no other enemies to encounter. We did not yet know that we had killed the first lieutenant of the cavalry, and that our opponents had retreated to the woods in dismay, without daring to return to their camp. This at least was the account we heard from prisoners afterwards, and was evidently the tale current in the neighborhood, though the statements published in Southern newspapers did not correspond. Admitting the death of Lieutenant Jones, the Tallahassee Floridian of February 14th stated that

"Captain Clark, finding the enemy in strong force, fell back with his command to camp, and removed his ordnance and commissary and other stores, with twelve negroes on their way to the enemy, captured on that day."

In the morning, my invaluable surgeon, Dr. Rogers, sent me his report of killed and wounded; and I have been since permitted to make the following extracts from his notes: "One man killed instantly by ball through the heart, and seven wounded, one of whom will die. Braver men never lived. One man with two bullet-holes through the large muscles of the shoulders and neck brought off from the scene of action, two miles distant, two muskets; and not a murmur has escaped his lips. Another, Robert Sutton, with three wounds,—one of which, being on the skull, may cost him his life,—would not report himself till compelled to do so by his officers. While dressing his wounds, he quietly talked of what they had done, and of what they yet could do. To-day I have had the Colonel *order* him to obey me. He is perfectly quiet and cool, but takes this whole affair with the religious bearing of a man who realizes that freedom is sweeter than life. Yet another soldier did not report himself at all, but remained all night on guard, and possibly I should not have known of his having had a buck-shot in his shoulder, if some duty requiring a sound shoulder had not been required of him to-day." This last, it may be added, had persuaded a comrade to dig out the buck-shot, for fear of being ordered on the sick-list. And one of those who were carried to the vessel—a man wounded through the lungs—asked only if I were safe, the contrary having been reported. An officer may be pardoned some enthusiasm for such men as these.

As the firing ceased and the smoke cleared away, I looked across the rice-fields which lay beneath the bluff.

The first sunbeams glowed upon their emerald levels, and on the blossoming hedges along the rectangular dikes. What were those black dots which everywhere appeared? Those moist meadows had become alive with human heads, and along each narrow path came a straggling file of men and women, all on a run for the riverside. I went ashore with a boat-load of troops at once. The landing was difficult and marshy. The astonished negroes tugged us up on the bank, and gazed on us as if we had been Cortez and Columbus. They kept arriving by land much faster than we could come by water; every moment increased the crowd, the jostling, the mutual clinging, on that miry foothold. What a scene it was! With the wild faces, eager figures, strange garments, it seemed, as one of the poor things reverently suggested, "like notin' but de judgment day." Presently they began to come from the houses also, with their little bundles on their heads; then with larger bundles. Old women, trotting on the narrow paths, would kneel to pray a little prayer, still balancing the bundle; and then would suddenly spring up, urged by the accumulating procession behind, and would move on till irresistibly compelled by thankfulness to dip down for another invocation. Reaching us, every human being must grasp our hands, amid exclamations of "Bress you, mas'r," and "Bress de Lord," at the rate of four of the latter ascriptions to one of the former. Women brought children on their shoulders; small black boys carried on their back little brothers equally inky, and, gravely depositing them, shook hands. Never had I seen human beings so clad, or rather so unclad, in such amazing squalidness and destitution of garments. I recall one small urchin without a rag of clothing save the basque waist of a lady's dress, bristling with whalebones, and worn wrong side before, beneath which his smooth ebony legs emerged like those of an ostrich from its plumage. How weak is imagination, how cold is memory, that I ever cease, for a day of my life, to see before me the picture of that astounding scene!

Yet at the time we were perforce a little impatient of all this piety, protestation, and hand-pressing; for the vital thing was to ascertain what force had been stationed at the bluff, and whether it was yet withdrawn. The slaves, on the other hand, were too much absorbed in their prospective freedom to aid us in taking any further steps to secure it. Captain Trowbridge, who had by this time landed at a different point, got quite into despair over the seeming deafness of the people to all questions. "How many soldiers are there on the bluff?" he asked of the first-comer.

"Mas'r," said the man, stuttering terribly, "I c-c-c—"

"Tell me how many soldiers there are!" roared Trowbridge, in his mighty voice, and all but shaking the poor old thing, in his thirst for information.

"O mas'r," recommenced in terror the incapacitated witness, "I c-c-carpenter!" holding up eagerly a little stump of a hatchet, his sole treasure, as if his profession ought to excuse him from all military opinions.

I wish that it were possible to present all this scene from the point of view of the slaves themselves. It can be most nearly done, perhaps, by quoting the description given of a similar scene on the Combahee River, by a very aged man, who had been brought down on the previous raid, already mentioned. I wrote it down in tent, long after, while the old man recited the tale, with much gesticulation, at the door; and it is by far the best glimpse I have ever had, through a negro's eyes, at these wonderful birthdays of freedom.

"De people was all a hoein', mas'r," said the old man.

"Dey was a hoein' in the rice-field, when de gunboats come. Den ebry man drap dem hoe, and leff de rice. De mas'r he stand and call, 'Run to de wood for hide! Yankee come, sell you to Cuba! run for hide!' Ebry man he run, and, my God! run all toder way!

"Mas'r stand in de wood, peep, peep, faid for truss [afraid to trust]. He say, 'Run to de wood!' and ebry man run by him, straight to de boat.

"De brack sojer so presumptious, dey come right ashore, hold up dere head. Fus' ting I know, dere was a barn, ten thousand bushel rough rice, all in a blaze, den mas'r's great house, all cracklin' up de roof. Didn't I keer for see 'em blaze? Lor, mas'r, didn't care notin' at all, *I was gwine to de boat.*"

Dore's Don Quixote could not surpass the sublime absorption in which the gaunt old man, with arm uplifted, described this state of affairs, till he ended in a shrewd chuckle, worthy of Sancho Panza. Then he resumed.

"De brack sojers so presumptious!" This he repeated three times, slowly shaking his head in an ecstasy of admiration. It flashed upon me that the apparition of a black soldier must amaze those still in bondage, much as a butterfly just from the chrysalis might astound his fellow-grubs. I inwardly vowed that my soldiers, at least, should be as "presumptious" as I could make them. Then he went on.

"Ole woman and I go down to de boat; den dey say behind us, 'Rebels comin'! Rebels comin'!' Ole woman say, 'Come ahead, come plenty ahead!' I hab notin' on but my shirt and pantaloon; ole woman one single frock he hab on, and one handkerchief on he head; I leff all-two my blanket and run for de Rebel come, and den dey didn't come, didn't truss for come.

"Ise eighty-eight year old, mas'r. My ole Mas'r Lowndes

keep all de ages in a big book, and when we come to age ob sense we mark 'em down ebry year, so I know. Too ole for come? Mas'r joking. Neber too ole for leave de land o' bondage. I old, but great good for chil'en, gib tousand tank ebry day. Young people can go through *force* [forcibly], mas'r, but de ole folk mus' go slow."

Such emotions as these, no doubt, were inspired by our arrival, but we could only hear their hasty utterance in passing; our duty being, with the small force already landed, to take possession of the bluff. Ascending, with proper precautions, the wooded hill, we soon found ourselves in the deserted camp of a light battery, amid scattered equipments and suggestions of a very unattractive breakfast. As soon as possible, skirmishers were thrown out through the woods to the farther edge of the bluff, while a party searched the houses, finding the usual large supply of furniture and pictures,—brought up for safety from below,—but no soldiers. Captain Trowbridge then got the *John Adams* beside the row of piles, and went to work for their removal.

Again I had the exciting sensation of being within the hostile lines,—the eager explorations, the doubts, the watchfulness, the listening for every sound of coming hoofs. Presently a horse's tread was heard in earnest, but it was a squad of our own men bringing in two captured cavalry soldiers. One of these, a sturdy fellow, submitted quietly to his lot, only begging that, whenever we should evacuate the bluff, a note should be left behind stating that he was a prisoner. The other, a very young man, and a member of the "Rebel Troop," a sort of Cadet corps among the Charleston youths, came to me in great wrath, complaining that the corporal of our squad had kicked him after he had surrendered. His air of offended pride was very rueful, and it did indeed seem a pathetic reversal of fortunes for the two races. To be sure, the youth was a scion of one of the foremost families of South Carolina, and when I considered the wrongs which the black race had encountered from those of his blood, first and last, it seemed as if the most scrupulous Recording Angel might tolerate one final kick to square the account. But I reproved the corporal, who respectfully disclaimed the charge, and said the kick was an incident of the scuffle. It certainly was not their habit to show such poor malice; they thought too well of themselves.

We who served with the black troops have this peculiar satisfaction, that, whatever dignity of sacredness the memories of the war may have to others, they have more to us. In that contest all the ordinary ties of patriotism were the same, of course, to us as to the rest; they had no motives which are not also ours. But the peculiar privilege of associating with an outcast race, of training it to defend its rights and to perform its duties, this was our especial need. The vacillating policy of the Government sometimes filled other officers with doubt and shame; until the negro had justice, they were but defending liberty with one hand and crushing it with the other. From this inconsistency we were free. Whatever the Government did, we at least were working in the right direction. If this was not recognized on our side of the lines, we knew that it was admitted on the other. Fighting with ropes round our necks, denied the ordinary courtesies of war till we ourselves compelled their concession, we could at least turn this outlawry into a compliment. We had touched the pivot of the war. Whether this vast dusky mass should prove the weakness of the nation or its strength, must depend in great measure, we knew, upon our efforts. Till the blacks were armed, there was no guaranty of their freedom. It was their demeanor under arms that shamed the nation into recognizing them as men.

6

"The Abduction of the Planter"
by Benjamin Quarles

*One of the outstanding military exploits of the Civil War
involved not a soldier, but a slave. Robert Smalls, some-
time waiter, teamster, and sailor, found himself aboard
the steamer* Planter *in the service of the Confederate
Navy at the beginning of the war. How he spirited the
ship out of Confederate waters and into the hands of the
Union forces is a delightful anecdote of the war. Smalls
was subsequently appointed second lieutenant piloting
the* Planter *for the Union navy for the duration of the
war.*

To the confederate capital on a spring afternoon in the
second year of the war came a one-sentence dispatch addressed to General R. E. Lee: "I have just learned by
telegraph that [the] steamer *Planter,* with five guns
aboard, intended for the harbor, was stolen in Charleston
this morning." Dated May 13, 1862, from the Savannah
headquarters of the Department of South Carolina and
Georgia, the terse report concluded with a "Very respectfully," and bore the name of the commanding officer,
J. C. Pemberton.

Pemberton's dispatch referred to the "abduction" by a
group of slaves of a Confederate vessel, a dramatic deed

which made its instigator, Robert Smalls, "an object of interest in Dupont's fleet," as Admiral David D. Porter phrased it. The spectacular escape of Smalls and his party became one of the war's oft-told stories. Requiring careful planning and brilliant execution, the feat in truth was unparalleled in audacity. "I thought," said Smalls, as he delivered the vessel to the Union Navy, "that the *Planter* might be of some use to Uncle Abe."

A native South Carolinian, Smalls was born in Beaufort in 1839. When he was twelve his master brought him to Charleston, where, after a succession of occupations, he finally became a rigger and began to learn boating and the twisting coastal waters. When the war came, the stockily built young slave was impressed into the Confederate service, and in March, 1862, he was made a member of the crew of the *Planter*.

Formerly a cotton steamer plying the Pee Dee River and capable of carrying 1400 bales, the *Planter* had been chartered by the war government and converted into a transport running from point to point in the Charleston harbor and the neighboring waters. Built of live oak and red cedar, the boat measured 150 feet in length, had a 30-foot beam, a depth of 7 feet 10 inches, and drew 3 feet 9 inches of water. As a Confederate dispatch boat, she mounted two guns for her own use, a 32-pounder pivot gun and a 24-pounder howitzer. Attached to the engineering department at Charleston, the *Planter* carried a crew of eleven, of whom three were whites—captain, mate, and engineer—and the remainder slaves.

By far the ablest of the slave crew was Smalls. Determined to escape, Smalls hit upon the idea of making off with the *Planter*. Wherever the Union Navy extended its blockade along the Southern seacoast, freedom-minded Negroes had sensed a new opportunity. By scow, oyster boat, barge, homemade canoe, or anything that would float, they made their way to the Union men-of-war. But no plan of escape was as imaginative and as daring as Smalls's.

The young wheelsman worked out the details in his mind. The escaping party would number sixteen, of whom half would be women and children, including Smalls's wife and their two young ones. The *Planter* would put out to sea casually, as though making a routine run to reconnoiter. Knowing they could expect little mercy if caught, Smalls bound the party to agree that if they were unable to make good their flight, they would blow up the vessel rather than be taken alive. Smalls's plan embraced one final but essential detail—all three white officers would have to remain ashore for the night. Such an absence would be contrary to standing general orders which stipulated that officers of light draft vessels were to remain "on board day and night" when their boat was docked at the wharf.

Finally came such a night as Smalls waited for—the night of May 12. Coincidentally, on the afternoon of that day, 200 pounds of ammunition and four guns—"a banded rifle 42, one 8-inch columbiad, one 8-inch sea-coast howitzer, and one 32-pounder"—had been loaded on the *Planter* for transport to the harbor battery, Fort Ripley.

With the white officers ashore, Smalls began to put his plan into operation. The sixteen slaves got aboard in the crisp early morning, the women and children being led below deck in pin-drop quiet. Smalls broke into Captain C. J. Relyea's cabin and took the captain's hat. At 3:00 A.M. one of the fugitives struck a match and set the kindlings on fire under the boilers; twenty-five minutes later the hawsers which moored the boat to Southern Wharf were cast off. From the pilothouse Smalls sounded the wharf signal. The shore sentinel at his post some fifty yards distant noticed the ship gliding away but sensed nothing afoot; he "did not think it necessary to stop her, presuming that she was but pursuing her usual business," in the language of an official report issued later that day.

Now to run the many fortifications in the harbor. Bristling with sea defenses, the defiant city was ringed with forts and batteries on constant alert. But for the runaway slaves there was no turning back. Hoisting the ship's two flags, Confederate and Palmetto, Smalls eased into the inner channel. He geared the *Planter* to its customary pace, although not to dash at full speed required the utmost self-control.

The critical minutes of the great deception had arrived. Wearing the captain's hat and mimicking his gait, Smalls stood in the pilothouse with the cord in his hand. As the vessel passed Fort Johnson, he pulled the lanyard on the steam whistle and gave the proper salute. All went well.

Finally the abductors approached the last hurdle, historic Fort Sumter. Thirteen months ago it was here that the opening shots of the war had been fired, and at the identical morning hour. One of the four transport guns on the *Planter* belonged originally, as Smalls well knew, to Fort Sumter, having been struck on the muzzle during the bombardment of that bastion and now having been repaired because of the Confederacy's scarcity of heavy guns.

Abreast of Sumter, Smalls sounded the private signal, three full whistles followed by a hissing one. "The sentinel on the parapet called for the corporal of the guard and reported the guard-boat going out," stated the official report of Major Alfred Rhett. In turn, the corporal of the guard relayed the intelligence to the officer of the day, Captain David G. Fleming. The information had been passed along in routine fashion since it was, in Major Rhett's words, "by no means unusual for the guard-boat to run out at that hour." Then Sumter answered, "All right." The *Planter* had been taken for the guard boat and hence allowed to pass!

The slave-manned steamer moved in a southeasterly direction and entered the main ship channel, maintaining her leisurely pace until she had out-distanced the line of fire of the Confederate battery. Then she got up steam, lowered her guns, and ran up a white flag.

Not a minute too soon was the flag of truce hoisted. Off Charleston was a Union blockading fleet of ten warships, and the *Planter* had been spied by the lookout on the inside ship, *Onward*. The commander, J. F. Nickels, had ordered his ship swung around so as to train the maximum gunfire on the approaching craft. Just as the *Onward* succeeded in bringing her port guns to bear on the oncoming steamer, Commander Nickels caught sight of the white flag. The gunners relaxed.

Unmolested, the harbor boat drew up alongside the armed sailing vessel. A prize crew boarded the *Planter* and greeted its crew. Down came the white flag, and up went the American ensign. Then and there in the outer harbor the ownership of the captive boat was transferred from the Confederate States of America to the Union Navy.

Later that morning the senior officer commanding the blockading squadron off Charleston, E. G. Parrott, taking advantage of the good weather, ordered the prize crew to take the *Planter* and its captors to Port Royal, and there to report the incident to Flag Officer S. F. Du Pont. No order could have pleased Smalls and his companions more, most of them having originally come from the Sea Island region.

The *Planter* made the sixty-mile trip to Port Royal by way of St. Helena Sound and Broad River, reaching her destination shortly after ten in the evening. Word awaited Smalls that he was to report directly to Du Pont, and the next morning he was ushered aboard the flagship *Wabash*. There the elderly admiral, "that stately and courteous potentate, elegant as one's ideal French marquis," listened attentively as the ex-slave told his story.

Later that day, in a lengthy report to the Secretary of the Navy, Du Pont summed up the exploit: "The bringing out of this steamer, under all the circumstances, would have done credit to anyone." The admiral also jotted down another conclusion: "This man, Robert Smalls, is superior to any who have yet come into the lines, intelligent as many of them have been."

Back in Charleston the news was received with consternation not unmingled with disbelief. In a front-page story devoted to the "extraordinary occurrence," the *Courier* reported that "our community was intensely agitated Tuesday morning by the intelligence that the steamer *Planter* . . . had been taken possession of by her colored crew, steamed up and boldly ran [sic] out to the blockaders." Added the daily, "The news was not at first credited." Another Charleston newspaper, the *Mercury,* concluded its descriptive story of the escape by explaining that "the run to Morris Island goes out a long way past the fort, and then turns. The *Planter* did not turn."

Voicing the general indignation of Confederate South Carolina over the negligence of the white officers of the boat, the *Columbia Guardian* expressed a fervent wish that the "recreant parties will be brought to speedy justice, and the prompt penalty of the halter rigorously enforced." From army headquarters in Richmond came a dispatch to General Pemberton stating that General Lee had received the papers relative to the *Planter's* escape and that "he very much regrets the circumstances, and hopes that necessary measures will be taken to prevent any repetition of a like misfortune."

News of Smalls's feat quickly spread throughout the North, and public sentiment became strong for awarding prize money to the *Planter's* crew. Congress responded, moving with unusual speed. Two weeks from the day of the seizure, that body passed a bill ordering the Secretary of the Navy to have the vessel appraised and "when the value thereof shall be thus ascertained to cause an equitable apportionment of one-half of such value . . . to be made between Robert Smalls and his associates who assisted in rescuing her from the enemies of the Government." Within another week Lincoln had signed the bill.

Smalls turned out to be right in believing that the *Planter* might be of some use to the North. Admirably suited to the shallow waters of the Sea Island region, she was immediately equipped with musket-proof bulwarks and converted into a navy transport, carrying upwards of seventy men. Exactly one month after the abduction, Admiral Du Pont, in acknowledging two letters from naval officer A. C. Rhind, wrote that he was "glad that the *Planter* has proved so useful a transport, and that we have again been able so materially to aid the army, especially at a critical time, when its generals were almost helpless for want of transports."

Early in September, 1862, the *Planter* was sold to the army, which could make much better use of a wood-burner than could the sister service. The quartermaster's department welcomed the addition, "as we have comparatively no vessels of light draft." Until she was decommissioned and sold at Baltimore in September, 1866, the *Planter* remained in military service, being used mainly as a troop transport, but seeing occasional service as a supply boat.

During most of its period of use by the armed forces, the *Planter* was piloted or commanded by Smalls. Over the four months the boat remained under navy supervision, the young Negro was employed as pilot. During the year 1863 and for the first two months in 1864, the army employed him in a like capacity, paying him $50 a month until September 30, 1863, then $75 a month from October 1 to November 30, 1863, and thenceforth $150 a month. On March 1, 1864, he was made captain.

The pilot was promoted to master as a reward for bravery under fire (before the war was over, Smalls had fought in seventeen engagements), but the appointment was merited on other grounds. For the fugitive slave brought much with him. His knowledge of the coastline of South Carolina and Georgia was intimate; few men were more familiar with the sinuous windings of those waters, and no hand was more skilled in their navigation. Indeed, "the accession of Smalls is deemed of more importance than the heavy guns of the *Planter*," wrote a reporter for the *Philadelphia Inquirer* (May 17, 1862), "as Smalls is thoroughly acquainted with all the intricacies of navigation in that region." Smalls also brought a knowledge of where the torpedoes had been planted to destroy the Union gunboats and where the masked batteries were located.

The intelligence he furnished was so valuable that the Secretary of the Navy, in his annual report to President Lincoln, made it a point to describe them:

> From information derived chiefly from the contraband Pilot, Robert Smalls, who has escaped from Charleston, Flag Officer Du Pont, after proper re-

connaissance, directed Commander Marchand to cross the bar with several gunboats and occupy Stono. The river was occupied as far as Legarville, and examinations extended further to ascertain the position of the enemy's batteries. The seizure of Stono Inlet and river secured an important base for military operations, and was virtually a turning of the forces in the Charleston harbor.

At the war's end Smalls was among the thousands who witnessed the re-raising of the American flag at Fort Sumter. This event had been scheduled for April 14, four years to the day after the one on which the Union forces had been forced to haul down the colors. Present at the flag-raising ceremonies was a distinguished roster of reformers and public notables, including William Lloyd Garrison, Judge Advocate General Joseph Holt, Supreme Court Justice N. H. Swayne, Senator Henry Wilson, and the chief speaker, Henry Ward Beecher. On hand also was Robert Anderson, brought back to Sumter to raise the very shot-pierced flag which the Southerners had forced him to lower four years previously. But perhaps the most symbolic figure present was Captain Robert Smalls, who that morning had left Charleston, Sumter bound, at the helm of the *Planter,* profusely decorated with the Stars and Stripes and loaded down with hundreds "of the emancipated race."

After the war Smalls had fifty years to live, many of them spent in the public eye—as a member of the South Carolina legislature, a five-term United States Congressman, and Collector of the Port at Beaufort. But no moment of his eventful life could ever match that memorable dawn when he abducted the *Planter.*

7

"A Soldier's Plea for Equal Pay"
by James Henry Gooding

The equality which Douglass and Higginson optimistically prophesied as a corollary to the formation of black regiments only slowly resulted after a bitter struggle within the army. Discriminated against from the start, Negro soldiers were given $10.00 a month with a $3.00 clothing deduction, while whites of similar rank were paid $13.00 plus a clothing allowance of $3.50. Two regiments, rather than accept less pay, refused to accept any money at all until they were paid and treated as equals. The hardships that this policy of discriminatory wages caused the Negro soldiers and their families is one of the shabbiest stories of the Civil War.

Finally, on June 15, 1864, Congress enacted legislation granting equal pay to Negro soldiers. It is unlikely that the following letter to President Lincoln was in any way responsible, but its pathos cannot be denied.

Your Excellency, Abraham Lincoln:
Your Excellency will pardon the presumption of a humble individual like myself in addressing you, but the earnest solicitation of my comrades in arms, besides the genuine interest felt by myself in the matter, is my ex-

cuse for placing before the executive head of the nation our common grievance.

On the 6th of the last month, the paymaster of the department informed us that if we would decide to receive the sum of $10 (ten dollars) per month, he would come and pay us that sum, but that, on the sitting of Congress, the regiment would, in his opinion, be allowed the other $3 (three). He did not give us any guarantee that this would be as he hoped; certainly *he* had no authority for making such guarantee, and we cannot suppose him acting in any way interested.

Now the main question is, are we *soldiers* or are we *laborers?* We are fully armed and equipped; have done all the various duties pertaining to a soldier's life; have conducted ourselves to the complete satisfaction of general officers who were, if any, prejudiced *against* us, but who now accord us all the encouragement and honor due us; have shared the perils and labor of reducing the first stronghold that flaunted a traitor flag; and more, Mr. President, today the Anglo-Saxon mother, wife, or sister are not alone in tears for departed sons, husbands, and brothers. The patient, trusting descendants of Africa's clime have dyed the ground with blood in defense of the Union and democracy. Men, too, Your Excellency, who know in a measure the cruelties of the iron heel of oppression, which, in years gone by, the very power their blood is now being spilled to maintain, ever ground them to the dust.

But when the war trumpet sounded o'er the land, when men knew not the friend from the traitor, the black man laid his life at the altar of the nation—and he was refused. When the arms of the Union were beaten, in the first year of the war, and the executive called for more food for its ravaging maw, again the black man begged the privilege of aiding his country in her need—to be again refused.

And now he is in the war, and how has he conducted himself? Let their dusky forms rise up out of the mires of James Island and give the answer. Let the rich mold around Wagner's parapets be upturned, and there will be found an eloquent answer. Obedient and patient and solid as a well are they. All we lack is a paler hue and a better acquaintance with the alphabet.

Now, Your Excellency, we have done a soldier's duty. Why can't we have a soldier's pay? You caution the Rebel chieftain that the United States knows no distinction in her soldiers. She insists on having all her soldiers of whatever creed or color to be treated according to the usages of war. Now, if the United States exacts uniformity of treatment of her soldiers from the insurgents, would it not be well and consistent to set the example herself by paying all her *soldiers* alike?

We of this regiment were not enlisted under any "contraband" act. But we do not wish to be understood as rating our service of more value to the government than the service of the ex-slave. Their service *is* undoubtedly worth much to the nation, but Congress made express provision touching their case, as slaves freed by military necessity, and assuming the government to be their temporary guardian. Not so with us. Freemen by birth and consequently having the advantage of *thinking* and acting for ourselves so far as the laws would allow us, we do not consider ourselves fit subjects for the contraband act.

We appeal to you, sir, as the executive of the nation, to have us justly dealt with. The regiment do pray that they be assured their service will be fairly appreciated by paying them as American *soldiers*, not as menial hirelings. Black men, you may well know, are poor; $3 per month, for a year, will supply their needy wives and assure us of our whole pay, we are content. Our patriotism, our enthusiasm will have a new impetus to exert our energy more and more to aid our country. Not that our hearts ever flagged in devotion, spite the evident apathy displayed in our behalf, but we feel as though our country spurned us, now we are sworn to serve her. Please give this a moment's attention.

8

FROM

The Buffalo Soldiers: A Narrative of the Negro Cavalry in the West *
by William Leckie

After the United States Colored Troops were disbanded at the end of the Civil War, Congress created several black volunteer units including two Cavalry regiments, the Ninth and Tenth. For the first time the nation's regular army accepted some 12,500 black peacetime volunteers. By 1871, all black regular troops were stationed at various posts in Texas and the Indian Territory. One out of every five of the mounted troopers in this area of the West was black, but it was not until 1877 that a Negro officer, Henry O. Flipper, the first black graduate from West Point, was assigned to the Tenth Cavalry.

The Indians themselves gave the name "Buffalo Soldiers" to the Negro men-in-arms in the West. It was partly because of their black skin and partly because of their toughness on the battlefield that they were so designated.

In the following chapter from The Buffalo Soldiers, *William Leckie describes what life was like for the men on the lonely frontier.*

By the close of the year the Ninth had seen nearly five years of the hardest kind of service with no respite. Most of the men had not seen their homes since enlistment, and efforts of the officers to secure extended furloughs for them were denied—at a high cost in veterans when enlistments expired. Their stations were among the most lonely and isolated to be found anywhere in the country, and mere service at such posts would seem to have called for honorable mention. Discipline was severe, food usually poor, recreation difficult, and violent death always near at hand. Prejudice robbed them of recognition and often even of simple justice.

A buffalo soldier in the Ninth could expect little mercy at the hands of a court-martial, even for trivial offenses. A dishonorable discharge and one year at hard labor was virtually automatic for drunkenness while on duty. The same sentence was the fate of Privates George Perry and Richard Talbot, both of Company I. Perry purloined a jar of candy from a saloon, while Talbot stole one dollar from a civilian. Private William Tolliver of A Company took a cat nap on guard duty and paid for his leisure with a stint of six months in the post guardhouse. Private John Curtis of H spent two months at hard labor for telling his sergeant to "go to hell" when ordered to help feed the company horses. The court was lenient with Private Andy Clayton of H, who was charged with entering the quarters of laundress Mrs. Lydia Brown, drawing a knife, and threatening, "I cut you if you don't undress and let me sleep with you." The verdict was "not guilty." Generally, however, the punishment meted out was more harsh than that in white regiments.

Poor meals, like poor horses, were constant companions of Negro troopers. The post surgeon at Fort Concho put it bluntly. The food was inferior to that provided in other posts. The bread was sour, beef of poor quality, and the canned peas not fit to eat. There were none of the

staples common at other posts—molasses, canned toma-
toes, dried apples, dried peaches, sauerkraut, potatoes,
onions. The butter was made of suet, and there was only
enough flour for the officers. Certainly there were no
visions of a sumptuous repast in the minds of worn-out
troopers coming in to Concho after days or weeks in the
field.

Off-post recreation, of a sort, was available in the sor-
did little towns that blossomed around the posts, but a
Negro soldier had no cause to seek trouble—it was awaiting him. If a trooper was unfortunate enough to lose his
life in a clash with a white citizen, his comrades could
hardly expect that justice would be served. One such
citizen, John Jackson, a settler near Fort McKavett, murdered a Negro infantryman, Private Boston Henry, in
cold blood, long eluded the law, and in the process shot
and killed Corporal Albert Marshall and Private Charles
Murray of Captain Carroll's F Company stationed at Fort
McKavett. When finally apprehended and brought to
trial, a jury quickly set him free.

Such conditions could have demoralized any regiment,
yet morale in the Ninth remained high. Desertion, the
curse of the frontier army, dwindled steadily to the point
that the rate was the lowest of any unit on the frontier.
Proud, tough, and confident, the Ninth was the equal of
any similar combat unit in the country, and it was well
that this was so for the most trying years were still in the
future.

Conditions on the Rio Grande, turbulent and bloody
for years, worsened in the eighteen seventies. . . .

Ill feeling and lack of co-operation hurt law-abiding
citizens on both sides of the river. In December a band
of American renegades attacked the small village of Res-
urrección in Mexico. As soon as the news reached Fort

Clark, Lieutenant Cusack and a strong detachment marched to the west bank of the Rio Grande opposite the village and managed by signals to induce the alcalde to come down to the riverbank. Cusack tried to obtain information about the raid by shouting across the river, but the alcalde's reply was so sarcastic that Cusack felt himself accused of having inspired the attack.

Revolutionaries were an increasing headache to the Ninth and kept patrols constantly on the lookout. Captain C. D. Beyer with Company C, working out to Fort McIntosh, should have received a decoration from the Mexican government, for he seemed to have a "nose for revolutionaries" and consistently located, arrested, and disarmed rebel leaders and their followers. In December he gathered up seven officers and thirty-seven privates in one swoop and learned that their commanding officer was in Mexico with an equal number of men. Beyer haunted the area for a week and had the pleasure of picking up a colonel and forty enlisted men.

General Augur probably spoke for every officer and man of the Ninth when he noted in his annual report for 1872:

> The labor and privations of troops in this Department are both severe. The cavalry particularly are constantly at work, and it is a kind of work too that disheartens, as there is very little to show for it. Yet their zeal is untiring, and if they do not always achieve success they always deserve it. I have never seen troops more constantly employed.

"Constantly employed" was an apt description of the buffalo soldiers and there were no indications of any change, for conditions along the Rio Grande did not improve

and Augur shifted five companies of the Ninth still farther downriver.

Colonel Hatch returned to his regiment in March,
1873, and established headquarters at Ringgold Barracks.
B, C, G, H, and L companies were quartered at Ringgold
with detachments thrown out for miles along the river
guarding crossings. Of necessity the other companies of
the regiment were scattered at Forts Concho, Stockton,
Davis, and McKavett to fend off Kiowa and Comanche
war parties to keep the El Paso road open.

Less than half a regiment supported by a few companies of infantry was woefully inadequate to cope with the
Rio Grande troubles, and while conditions on the north-
western frontier of Texas were far from satisfactory,
Augur, after conferences with General Sheridan, transferred the Fourth Cavalry to Fort Clark. In April, Colonel Mackenzie was apparently given carte blanche to
cross the Rio Grande if, in his opinion, circumstances
warranted such action. On May 16, Mackenzie received
word that a fresh trail had been discovered near the river,
and he set out at once from Fort Clark with six companies of his regiment, a detachment of the Twenty-fourth
Infantry, and a few scouts.

The trail led to the Rio Grande which was crossed and
the pursuit continued into Mexico. Early on the morning
of May 18 Mackenzie surprised and destroyed three Indian villages, killing nineteen warriors, capturing forty
women and children and the Lipan chief, Castillitos,
along with sixty-five ponies. Mackenzie was back at Fort
Clark before surprised Mexican officials could move to
intercept him, and strong protests by their government
failed to move President Grant who supported his vigor-
ous commander.

Augur reported optimistically that Mackenzie's raid

had done much to quiet the Rio Grande frontier, but this was hardly the case. A single raid, nineteen dead Indians, and a few captives scarcely brought a new order of things. If so, the buffalo soldiers—who had longed to make just such a raid—failed to feel or perceive it. There were many times more than nineteen Indians, bandits, and white renegades infesting the border—more than enough to keep the troopers in the saddle from morning until night—and they were still not permitted to cross that frustrating ribbon of water to overhaul their tormentors.

For two more long, grim, and frustrating years Hatch and nearly half his regiment sought to bring peace and order to a tortured frontier, and they did succeed in cutting down on cattle losses and breaking up bands of outlaws, but conditions remained so bad as to defy description. The country for thirty miles back from the river was a brush jungle and the population was almost entirely Mexican, with these people living on either side of the Rio Grande as convenience or necessity suited them. Small parties organized, stole, killed, plundered, and swiftly dispersed. Such lawlessness was almost impossible to prevent, and spies were everywhere reporting on the location and movement of troops. And, in this witches' brew, the marauding Indian was never far away.

Detachments of the Ninth could not be everywhere, but to their everlasting credit they tried. Patrols moved from ranch to ranch, from river crossing to river crossing in constant motion. Others were stationed at or near the small border towns where the "deputy collectors could not stay a day without troops at those places." When raiders were caught, there was no guarantee of punishment, for local juries showed a decided preference for a verdict of "not guilty."

The Ninth's effectiveness was in no small measure hampered by harassment from local officials who disliked anything in a blue uniform, particularly if Negroes wore that uniform. Among minor nuisances at Fort Ringgold were professional gamblers who infested the post on paydays to relieve the men of their earnings. Hatch was determined to stop the practice and in December, 1874, had post guards bring one member of the gambling fraternity, a Mr. James Johnson, to his office. Hatch delivered a tongue-lashing and ordered this somewhat dubious pillar of the community off the post.

Promptly, a Starr County grand jury indicted Hatch for "false imprisonment" and he was forced to retain a lawyer to quash the indictment. The attorney general's office refused to countenance payment of the legal fees and Hatch found himself faced with a suit by his erstwhile legal counsel for five hundred dollars.

Far more serious was an affair the following month. On the evening of January 26, 1875, Sergeant Edward Troutman and four privates of G Company, on patrol out of Ringgold, encamped near the Solis ranch house some sixteen miles from their post. As the troopers prepared their supper, bullets whistled near their heads. Believing the shots had come from the ranch house, Troutman approached and questioned a number of men lounging about. He received evasive answers, noticed the men were all heavily armed, and returned to his camp.

After discussing the situation with his fellow troopers, Troutman ordered them to mount and move off. They had traveled only a short distance when they were fired upon from ambush. A vicious short-range fight ensued in which Privates Jerry Owsley and Moses Turner were killed, Privates Charley Blackstone and John Fredericks managed to escape into the brush, and Troutman fought his way out of the ambush and made his way back to

Ringgold. Troutman believed his patrol had killed at least one man and wounded several others.

Early next morning, an angry Hatch, with sixty troopers from B and G companies and Deputy Sheriff T. Davis, marched to the scene of the attack and found the horribly mutilated bodies of Owsley and Turner. In a shack nearby, the uniforms and other equipment of the slain men were found. Hatch then moved on to the ranch house and "arrested every suspicious character I could find." Two of those arrested were suffering from bullet wounds. A grand jury at Rio Grande City indicted nine Mexicans for the murders, but only one was tried and quickly acquitted. The remaining eight were permitted to go free.

The affair did not end here, however, for troopers Troutman, Blackstone, and Fredericks, in Rio Grande City to testify for the prosecution, found themselves in arrest and under indictment for murder of one of their attackers. Shortly thereafter Hatch and Lieutenant J. H. French were also indicted—for burglary. They had illegally entered the shack from which they had taken the effects of the murdered Owsley and Turner! Starr County, Texas, took excellent care of its own.

Hatch, French, and the three troopers were eventually cleared of the charges against them, but were forced to employ legal counsel and obtain a change of venue to do so. According to their attorney, Stephen Powers, malice in the area toward Hatch and his men was very great and their indictments stemmed from "gratification of purely local prejudice." If the army high command drew a "water line" for the Ninth, it was also true that the people of the border drew a "color line. . . ."

At this point, General Augur was replaced by General E.O.C. Ord, the latter under instructions not to disperse his troops in small detachments, but to keep them at posts in at least company strength. Sherman believed that Ord should call upon sheriffs and local citizens to form posses and send word immediately to military posts as quickly as they discovered that raiders were in the vicinity. Sherman had a lot to learn about co-operation from citizens along the river.

Governor Coke had a far more realistic view of how to cope with the situation. He pleaded with President Grant to permit troops to cross into Mexico in pursuit of raiders and punish them wherever caught. Ord agreed with Coke, but received unequivocal instructions that no troops were to cross the river without express permission from Washington.

Meanwhile, disgusted with lack of local co-operation on the lower river, Secretary of War William Belknap telegraphed Governor Coke that if harassment of federal forces by civil authorities did not stop, he would remove all troops "from that locality." And, to lend weight to the threat, Hatch was ordered to transfer his headquarters to Fort Clark and "draw in" outlying companies from Fort Ringgold. These moves proved a preliminary to transfer of the Ninth from Texas. Sheridan wrote his superiors that the time had come to give officers and men of the regiment some relief. For eight years they had garrisoned the worst posts on the frontier and carried out their duties under the most trying conditions. As a result, Hatch received orders in September, 1875, transferring the regiment to the District of New Mexico. The Eighth Cavalry took its place along the river and soon had the privilege denied the men of the Ninth—permission to cross the Rio Grande in "hot pursuit" of marauders.

9

FROM

*The Colored Regulars in
the United States Army*

by Theophilas G. Steward
(1843–1925)

Everyone remembers the sinking of the Maine. *What
hardly anyone knows is that twenty-two of the crew members who perished were black. After war was declared
against Spain on April 13, 1898, black regiments landed
in Cuba in the midst of the fighting and won laurels for
their valor at El Caney. White southern soldiers were
quick to praise their comrades in arms, and initially
Teddy Roosevelt had only good things to say about the
"smoked Yankees." Roosevelt's memory was short, however, and less than a year later he would say, "They are,
of course, peculiarly dependent on their white officers."*

*The turn of the century saw the status of the Negro in-
creasingly threatened, both in military service and in civilian life. Discrimination deprived many brave men of
recognition, as Theophilas Steward relates in the following pages.*

The Twenty-fourth Infantry . . . reached the crest of
the San Juan Hills in such numbers as to lead the press
correspondents and others to conclude that there were
more men of this regiment promptly on the ground than

of any other one regiment. It is certain they made a record for heroism in that assault as bright as any won on the field that day, and this record they raised to a magnificent climax by their subsequent work in the fever hospital at Siboney. For their distinguished service both in the field and in the hospital, the colored ladies of New York honored themselves in presenting the regiment the beautiful stand of colors. . . .

Thus these four colored regiments took their place on the march, in camp, in assault and in siege with the flower of the American Army, the choice and pick of the American nation, and came off acknowledged as having shared equally in heroism and sacrifices with the other regular regiments so engaged, and deserving of special mention for the exhibition of regard for the welfare of their fellow man. The query is now pertinent as to the return which has been made to these brave men. The question of Ahasuerus when told of the valuable services of the Jew, Mordecai, is the question which the better nature of the whole American people should ask on hearing the general report of the valuable services of the Negro Regular in the Spanish War. When Ahasuerus asked: "What honor and dignity hath been done to Mordecai for this?" his servants that ministered unto him were compelled to answer: "There is nothing done for him." Looking over these four regiments at the time of this writing an answer somewhat similar in force must be returned. That the colored soldier is entitled to honor and dignity must be admitted by all who admire brave deeds, or regard the welfare of the state. The colored soldier, however, was compelled to stand by and see a hundred lieutenancies filled in the Regular Army, many in his own regiments, only to find himself overlooked and to be forced to feel that his services however valuable, could not outweigh the demerit of his complexion.

The sum total of permanent advantage secured to the colored regular as such, in that bloody ordeal where brave men gave up their lives for their country's honor, consists of a few certificates of merit entitling the holders to two dollars per month additional pay as long as they remain in the service. Nor is this all, or even the worst of the matter. Men who served in the war as First Sergeants, and who distinguished themselves in that capacity, have been allowed to go back to their old companies to serve in inferior positions. . . .

It must not be inferred from the foregoing, however, that nothing whatever was done in recognition of the gallantry of the colored regulars. Something was done. Cases of individual heroism were so marked, and so numerous, that they could not be ignored. The men who had so distinguished themselves could not be disposed of by special mention and compliments in orders. Something more substantial was required. Fortunately for such purposes four regiments of colored United States Volunteer Infantry were then in course of organization, in which the policy had been established that colored men should be accepted as officers below the grade of captain. Into these regiments the colored men who had won distinction at Santiago were placed, many as Second Lieutenants, although some were given First Lieutenancies. This action of the Government was hailed with great delight on the part of the colored Americans generally, and the honors were accepted very gratefully by the soldiers who had won them on the field. Fortunately as this opening seemed, it turned out very disappointing. It soon became evident that these regiments would be mustered out of the service, as they had proven themselves no more immune, so far as it could be determined from the facts, than other troops. The Lieutenants who had been most fortunate in getting their commissions early got about six or seven months' service, and then the dream of their glory departed and they fell back to the ranks to stand "attention" to any white man who could muster political influence sufficient to secure a commission. Their day was short, and when they were discharged from the volunteer service, there appeared no future for them as commissioned officers. Their occupation was indeed gone. It was for them a most disappointing and exasperating promotion, resulting in some cases in loss of standing and in financial injury. Their honors were too short-lived, and too circumscribed, to be much more than a lively tantalization, to be remembered with disgust by those who had worn them. Cruel, indeed, was the prejudice that could dictate such a policy to the brave black men of San Juan. The black heroes, however, were not without sympathy in their misfortune. The good people of the country had still a warm place in their hearts for the colored soldier, despite the sayings of his maligners.

The people of Washington, D. C., had an opportunity to testify their appreciation of the Tenth Cavalry as that regiment passed through their city on its way to its station in Alabama, and later a portion of it was called to Philadelphia to take part in the Peace Jubilee, and no troops received more generous attention. To express in some lasting form their regard for the regiment and its officers, some patriotic citizens of Philadelphia presented a handsome saber to Captain Charles G. Ayres, who had charge of the detachment which took part in the Peace Jubilee, "as a token of their appreciation of the splendid conduct of the regiment in the campaign of Santiago, and of its superb soldierly appearance and good conduct during its attendance at the Jubilee Parade in Philadelphia."

Likewise when the Twenty-fifth Infantry arrived at its station at Fort Logan, Colorado, the people of Denver gave to both officers and men a most cordial reception, and invited them at once to take part in their fall carnival. All over the country there was at that time an unusual degree of good feeling toward the colored soldier who had fought so well, and no one seemed to begrudge him the rest which came to him or the honors bestowed upon him.

This state of feeling did not last. Before the year closed assiduous efforts were made to poison the public mind toward the black soldier, and history can but record that these efforts were too successful. The three hundred colored officers became an object of which both prejudice and jealousy could strike; but to reach them the reputation of the entire colored contingent must be assailed. This was done with such vehemence and persistency that by the opening of 1899 the good name of the black regular was hidden under the rubbish of reports of misconduct. So much had been said and done, even in Denver, which had poured out its welcome words to the heroes of El Caney, that the Ministerial Alliance of that city, on February 6, 1899, found it necessary to take up the subject, and that body expressed itself in the unanimous adoption of the following resolutions:

RESOLUTIONS ADOPTED UNANIMOUSLY BY THE MINISTERIAL ALLIANCE OF DENVER, FEBRUARY 6, 1899.

Resolved, By the Ministerial Alliance of the City of Denver, that the attempt made in certain quarters to have the Twenty-fifth Regiment, United States Infantry, removed from Fort Logan, appears to this body to rest on no just grounds, to be animated on the contrary by motives unworthy and discreditable to Denver and the State, and that especially in view of the heroic record of the Twenty-fifth Regiment, its presence here is an honor to Denver and Colorado, which this Alliance would regret to have withdrawn.

The mustering out of the volunteers about the time this opposition was approaching what appeared to be a climax, causing the removal from the service of the colored officers, appeased the wrath of the demon, and the waves of the storm gradually sank to a peace, gratifying, indeed, to those who shuddered to see a black man with shoulder-straps. As the last Negro officer descended from the platform and honorably laid aside his sword to take his place as a citizen of the Republic, or a private in her armies, that class of our citizenship breathed a sigh of relief. What mattered it to them whether justice were done; whether the army were weakened; whether individuals were wronged; they were relieved from seeing Negroes in officers' uniforms, and that to them is a most gracious portion. The discharge of the volunteers was to them the triumph of their prejudices, and in it they took great comfort, although as a matter of fact it was a plain national movement coming about as a logical sequence, entirely independent of their whims or wishes. The injustice to the Negro officer does not lie in his being mustered out of the volunteer service, but in the failure to provide for a recognition of his valor in the nation's permanent military establishment.

The departure of the colored man from the volunteer service was the consequent disappearance of the colored military officer, with the single exception of Lieutenant Charles Young of the Regular Cavalry, had a very depressing effect upon the colored people at large, and called forth from their press and their associations most earnest protests. With a few exceptions, these protests were encouched in respectful language toward the President and his advisers, but the grounds upon which they were based were so fair and just, that right-thinking men could not avoid their force. The following resolution, passed by the National Afro-American Council, may be taken as representative of the best form of such remonstrance:

> "*Resolved,* That we are heartily grieved that the President of the United States and those in authority have not from time to time used their high station to voice the best conscience of the nation in regard to mob violence and fair treatment of justly deserving men. It is not right that American citizens should be despoiled of life and liberty while the nation looks silently on; or that soldiers who, with conspicuous bravery, offer their lives for the country, should have their promotion result in practical dismissal from the army."

The nation graciously heeded the call of justice and in the reorganization of the volunteer army provided for two colored regiments, of which all the company officers should be colored men. Under this arrangement many of the black heroes of Santiago were recalled from the ranks and again restored to the positions they had won. Thus did the nation in part remedy the evil which came in consequence of the discharge of the volunteers, and prove its willingness to do right. Triumphantly did the Administration vindicate itself in the eyes of good people, and again did it place its withering disapproval upon the conduct of those who were ready to shout their applause over the worthy black officer's accidental humiliation. The Negro officer disappeared from the United States' Regiments as a Lieutenant only; but he returns to the same, or rather, to a higher grade of the same form of regiments, both as Lieutenant and Captain. How rapid and pronounced has been the evolution! It is true the Negro officer is still a volunteer, but his standing is measurably improved, both because of the fact of his recall, and also because the regiments which he is now entering have some prospect of being incorporated into the Regular Army. It does not seem probable that the nation can much longer postpone the increase of the standing army, and in this increase it is to be hoped the American Negro, both as soldier and officer, will receive that full measure of justice of which the formation of the present two colored regiments is so conspicuous a part.

10

FROM

From Harlem to the Rhine

by Arthur Little

At the beginning of World War I there were approximately 20,000 Negroes out of a total of 750,000 men in the Regular Army and the National Guard. Although blacks thronged the recruiting stations in great numbers in April, 1917, few were accepted by Uncle Sam. A month later, however, the Selective Service Act was passed enabling (in theory, at least) all able-bodied Americans between the ages of twenty-one and thirty-one to enlist.

Negroes were particularly anxious to participate in the war as officers, and as agitation finally overcame opposition, separate officers training camps were formed for Negro soldiers.

Racial tensions were particularly high during the war years. Southerners greatly objected to training camps for black soldiers, especially black soldiers from the North, on southern soil. The Negro soldiers and sailors who were fighting to make the world safe for democracy were verbally and physically abused by their fellow Americans at home. More than one admitted he had been better treated in Europe.

Black Americans fought heroically in Europe and gained the respect of European military personnel. One of the most sensational feats of the war was performed by Privates Henry Johnson and Needham Roberts, both

*members of the 369th Infantry, a black regiment. The
company commander, Arthur Little, relates the circumstances in the following chapter from* From Harlem to
the Rhine.

Upon October 8th, 1917, the regiment left its stations in
and near New York to journey to Spartanburg, South
Carolina. Special trains were arranged for each battalion,
and for Headquarters and Supply companies combined.

Col. Hayward, the Regimental Surgeon Major Whitte-
more, Captain Hinton, Supply Officer, and I traveled by
regular express train—making the trip in about twenty-
two hours, and arriving in Spartanburg nearly three days
ahead of the troop trains.

The sanguinary affair of the 24th Infantry (colored) at
Houston, Texas, was still occupying prominent newspaper space. It may be recalled that, stirred to action by
a sense of grievance over grave injustices based upon
Southern feeling between the white population and the
colored people, a serious breach of the peace had occurred during the last week of August, 1917. A considerable body of colored soldiers had violated the discipline
of their command by breaking out of camp, invading the
city, and, armed with service rifles and ammunition—
"shooting up" the town. Seventeen deaths of citizens and
more than a score of woundings were reported. An officer
(Captain J. W. Mattes) who had attempted by power of
command to bring the riotous soldiers to order, had been
shot and killed.

During the height of the excitement founded upon the
explosion of the mutinous element of the 24th Infantry,
the War Department ordered the 15th N. Y. Inf. N. G.
(colored) to Camp Wadsworth, at Spartanburg, South
Carolina.

Immediately following the publication of the orders, Mr. and Mrs. Worry and Mr. and Mrs. Trouble-Hunter, and all of the relatives and friends of these leading families of Spartanburg, South Carolina, organized to arrange for the reception of our distinguished regiment—which was entirely peaceable in its aims, purposes, and ideals towards the world—except the Kaiser.

Upon August 31st, the New York *Times* had published the following news item from Spartanburg.

Camp Wadsworth, Spartanburg, S. C., Aug. 30, 1917.

Following the receipt of a report that the Government intended to alter its original plan and include the Fifteenth Infantry, colored, in the troops to be trained at the camp here, the City of Spartanburg officially protested to the War Department against the sending of these troops, on the ground that trouble might result if the Fifteenth refused to accept the limited liberties accorded to the city's colored population. Mayor J. F. Floyd, in his protest, called attention to the recent outbreak of negro troops at Houston, Texas.

That Colonel William B. Hayward's organization, one of the first of the city's regiments to reach its war strength, is unwelcome here is evident from the comments heard in the streets. The whites here are outspoken in their opposition to the plan and predict trouble if the War Department fails to heed the protest.

"I was sorry to learn that the Fifteenth Regiment has been ordered here," said Mayor Floyd to-night, "for, with their northern ideas about race equality, they will probably expect to be treated like white men. I can say right here that they will not be treated as anything except negroes. We shall treat them exactly as we treat our resident negroes. This thing is like waving a red flag in the face of a bull, something that can't be done without trouble. We have asked Congressman Nicholls to request the War Department not to send the soldiers here. You remember the trouble a couple of weeks ago at Houston."

Chamber of Commerce Objects

While the sentiment against the Fifteenth extended through all classes in the city, the opposition took form through the Chamber of Commerce, which put the matter before the Mayor.

"We asked for the camp at Spartanburg," said an official of the Chamber this afternoon, "but at that time we understood that no colored troops were to be sent down. It is a great mistake to send Northern negroes down here, for they do not understand our attitude. We wouldn't mind it if the Government sent us a regiment of Southern negroes; we understand them and they understand us. But with those Northern fellows it's different.

"I can tell you for certain that if any of those colored soldiers go in any of our soda stores and the like and ask to be served they'll be knocked down. Somebody will throw a bottle. We don't allow negroes to use the same glass that a white man may later have to drink out of. We have our customs down here, and we aren't going to alter them."

It was suggested that the Fifteenth might make an appeal on its own behalf to the military authorities at the camp. The reply was to the effect that it would be futile for the military authorities to attempt to regulate the customs of the country, and that the situation would simply have to be accepted. No attempt, it was said, would be made to alleviate things by the establishment of "Jim Crow" soda stores or restaurants, because there are already a number of such enterprises devoted exclusively to the negroes.

These shops, however, visited by newspaper men, proved to be almost without exception dingy and poorly stocked. It is believed that the soldiers will not be satisfied with these shops and will try to get something better.

In the event that the Fifteenth does come here, it is planned to send a committee of citizens to call upon Major Gen. O'Ryan and ask him to explain to the negro soldiers the difference between South Carolina and New York City. Then, if the Fifteenth is willing to accept the order of things, all will be well; if they chafe under the restriction, "the customs will be observed just the same."

Plans to Welcome Division

As for the other members of the 27th Division, Spartanburg and the big camp to-night are ready and waiting for them. It is figured here that about thirty hours will be required for the troop trains to reach here. At the camp the regimental camp sites have all been staked out, sanitary arrangements have been completed by a special detail of 107 men from the regular army Medical Service, and it is estimated that it will be possible to put three full brigades under canvas and thoroughly "settle" them within two hours after arrival. At camp headquarters the belief is that a much larger part of the division will be in camp by Monday night than was at first planned.

The 30,000 inhabitants of this city have been planning for weeks to welcome the New Yorkers, and with the report that several of the units would depart from New York to-night, the folks are having a hard time restraining themselves from going down to the railroad station and camping there so as to be sure to be on hand when the troop trains get in.

That challenge or threat by Mayor Floyd was discussed generally and freely throughout our regiment. And the old rule of trouble hunters usually being successful in their quests was in a fair way of being justified.

After many hardships at sea the 369th United States Infantry arrived in France and in April, 1918, moved up to the front lines.

Upon May 11th, 1918, the 1st Battalion relieved the 2nd Battalion in the C. R. Montplaisir. The 2nd Battalion went to Maffreecourt for its ten days of rest and training.

Montplaisir was the center of resistance in which our 1st Battalion men had doubled for four or five days with the French Battalion Josse, during our first tour in the trenches. We were, therefore, more or less at home, we knew the terrain and the trenches. We also knew of weaknesses in the organization of the combat groups. This knowledge explained to us an uncomfortable experience of the first night of our second tour—by enemy sniping from the rear of the positions of our observation posts.

By daylight inspection we discovered points upon the front line at which entrance to the sector could be effected with comparative ease. We also found abandoned dugouts which showed signs of having been occupied by snipers.

The dugouts (and hiding places) we set about destroying. At the weak points in the line, we established ambuscades or rather, planned a series of ambuscades to be operated in rotation.

Upon the night of May 12th–13th, we had three parties out all night waiting for the enemy invaders. The entire battalion was keyed up to intense interest and hope. There seemed to us to be almost a certainty of contact, with excellent chances of success by the taking of prisoners. Captain MacClinton commanded one party, Lieutenant Webb commanded another. The third ambuscade, I, myself, commanded.

Slowly, the hours of the night wore away. The stillness was oppressive. A smothered cough or the snore of a dozing soldier, the whispered reproof of a non-com or the prod of a wide awake side partner, were sounds that seemed as if they must carry clear over the enemy trenches. Frequently, suspicious incoming sounds would cause us to strain eyes and ears. Such sounds were usually answered from our combat groups, stretched out to either side of us, over a long line of irregularity, by illuminating rockets—sometimes by the fire of automatic rifles and defensive grenades.

We saw the moon travel its complete course of the night, at first bringing out of pitch darkness sharply defined paths of beams and shadows, changing this great gridiron into a broad plain of beautifully soft but uncertain light, and sinking into the opposite side of the world from that upon which it had made its appearance—the light over the plain changing, through many shades of purple, once more into darkness to be awakened again after a few minutes of slumber by a gray lightning, followed quickly by the rays of the rising sun.

With each of the changes of the night we had our alarms, our thrills—our hopes; but that was all we had. We made no contact. We took no prisoners.

Just before broad daylight, while the troops of the entire battalion were "Standing-to" at their posts, through every line of the sector—observation, resistance, and redoubt—we crawled into the trenches, and wearily made our way back to quarters—and to sleep.

The next night, the night of the 13th–14th of May three other ambuscades were set—at other points and with other personnel.

At about half past two in the morning, at the point where my party had lain all the night before, the Germans came. There were no Americans there to meet them that night, however, and the Boche were able to make their way in peace, a hundred and fifty yards or more to the west, to the rear of Combat Group No. 29.

Number 29 was a tiny post, actually isolated, but theoretically a part of number 28, some fifty or sixty yards still farther to the West.

Number 28 was garrisoned by a strong force, of at least half a platoon, under command of an officer, Lieutenant Richardson Pratt of Brooklyn.

Number 29 was manned by four men and a corporal. The post was but little more than an islet of observation. Its armament had no automatic rifles. It was a part of the command of the officer stationed at Number 28.

As the enemy patrol made its way cautiously through the field of wire that protected the rear of Number 29 from rushing tactics, some slight sound (probably that of the functioning of a wire clipper) arrested the attention of Private Needham Roberts, on guard at the east side of the enclosure. Roberts slipped over to the other side, and, cautioning his partner of the relief, Private Henry Johnson, for silence, led him back to the spot where the noise had been heard.

Together the boys listened and peered. Presently that sound was repeated.

An illuminating rocket was discharged into the field from which the sound came, and, "Corporal of the Guard!" was shouted at the top of the voices of the two plucky little volunteers—Roberts of Trenton, N. J., and Johnson of Albany, N. Y.

The signal of discovery was the signal for attack—for the Germans. Quickly and without further caution the wire clippers worked. A volley of grenades was thrown into the little fortified area of Combat Group No. 29, and both Roberts and Johnson were wounded. The Corporal and the off relief of two men, sleeping in the dugout, were penned in.

Roberts, badly hurt and unable to rise, propped himself against the door of the dugout and threw grenades out into the darkness.

Johnson was back on his feet, rifle in hand, in time to meet the rush of the Germans as they came piling into the enclosure.

The Labelle rifle carries a magazine clip of but three cartridges. Johnson fired his three shots—the last one almost muzzle to breast of the Boche bearing down upon him. As the German fell, a comrade jumped over his body, pistol in hand, to avenge his death.

There was no time for reloading. Johnson swung his rifle round his head, and brought it down with a thrown blow upon the head of the German. The German went down, crying, in perfectly good Bowery English, "The little black so and so has got me!"

"Yas, an' dis little black so so'll git yer 'gin—ef yer git up!" went back the high pitched voice of Henry Johnson, in admirable repartee, as he varied, for a few seconds, the monotonous call for the Corporal of the Guard which he kept repeating, between the grunts of his exertions, all through the fight.

With the enemy in the front for the moment disposed

of, Johnson glanced over his shoulder to the left, to see how things were going with his partner. Two Germans had lifted Roberts from the ground, one had him by the shoulders and one by the feet, and they were about to rise, to carry him away—a prisoner.

Our men were unanimous in the opinion that death was to be preferred to a German prison. But Johnson was of the opinion that victory was to be preferred to either.

With side spring, the active little soldier from Albany came down like a wildcat upon the shoulders of the German with the head of Roberts between his knees. As Johnson sprang, he unsheathed his bolo knife, and as his knees landed upon the shoulders of that ill-fated Boche, the blade of the knife was buried to the hilt through the crown of the German's head.

A bolo knife weighs no less than three pounds. The blade is at least eight or nine inches in length. The Germans upon patrol wear no helmets, presumably upon the theory that the danger of noise from the striking against them of wire is greater than the danger of wounds owing to lack of protection to the head. One of the war relics of the 16th Division of France, valued by General Le Gallais as a memento of the world-famous fight of his little American soldier, is the gray cloth, red bound round cap of that short-lived captor of Needham Roberts. Through the crown of the cap is a clean-cut slit about two and a half inches in width. Glued to the lining of the cap, glued by blood of its owner, is a thick lock of brown hair.

Johnson turned once more to the front. He was none too soon. The Boche who had been knocked down by clubbed rifle was up! He was up and mad—fighting mad. Down upon the plucky little Johnson he bore—his Lueger automatic pistol spitting a stream of fire as he charged. Johnson felt a burning, stinging pain. He cried out as if in despair; and dropped upon hands and knees. The German closed in. The next instant Johnson was up and under the guard of the German; and that terrible bolo knife was in the German's abdomen. Johnson showed no quarter. The knife was turned. The enemy soldier was disembowelled.

The enemy patrol was in a panic. The dead and wounded were piled upon stretchers and carried away.

When daylight came, we trailed the course of the enemy retreat (a roundabout course of at least a half mile through the woods) to the back of the river, where they crossed. We trailed the course with the greatest of ease, by pools of blood, blood-soaked handkerchiefs and first aid bandages, and blood-smeared logs, where the routed party had rested.

Johnson was wounded in many places. He was almost exhausted. He seemed to know by instinct, however, that the mere turning point of a battle is not the time for the victor to suspend hostilities. The enemy was retreating. Certainty must be made that it should never come back.

As the Germans piled through the chicane which they had cut in our wire, Johnson pelted them with grenades. We found evidence that at least one man had been terribly torn by the iron of these explosions. At the narrowest point in the opening, where they could do no better than go in single file, was found a terrible mass of flesh and blood, and the cloth of a coat, and the pulped material of a first aid packet—blown open. Upon the ground, in this opening, was the shell hole blown by the grenade. The hole was of the size and shape of a five gallon punch bowl; and it was almost filled with thick, sticky blood. In the Champagne country, the soil is of a chalky clay, of a quality to hold water for very slow absorption. The blood of that grenade-blown punch bowl was not wholly absorbed for more than a week.

As the relief-party, headed by Lieutenant Pratt, entered the enclosure of Combat Group Number 29, Henry Johnson fainted. As he passed out, he mumbled the words —"Corporal of the Guard!"

The first news that I received of "The Battle of Henry Johnson" was brought to me by Sergeant-Major Hooper, at about 3:30 in the morning.

Hooper entered my cabin and reported that there had been a fight in the left P.C. (*point d'apuis*); that no official report had as yet come down; but that two wounded men (probably dying) had just passed our headquarters upon a flat-car of the mule-power railroad line, to be taken to the sector dressing station, and to wait for an ambulance, which had been ordered.

A pair of rubber boots and a raincoat over my pajamas was the bill of dress in which I raced after that flat-car.

When I reached the dressing station, both men were conscious, and not only able but glad to talk. Captain MacClinton, in evacuating the men after the administering of first aid, had given to each a cup full of the rum which is always kept for emergencies at the company commander's P.C., in front line sectors.

Both Roberts and Johnson were remarkably coherent in their statements. It was the first fight we'd had in the regiment, and the first of our casualties. I feared that these men would die. They were wounded in so many places. I suppose my face must have shown emotional concern. I finished my note making and pocketed my book, just as the ambulance arrived.

Henry Johnson looked up at me and motioned that he had something more to say. I knelt at his side.

"Suh Cap'n Suh," said the wounded hero, in a low, husky voice, but with an indescribably gentle smile, "Suh Cap'n Suh, yoo all doan' want er worry 'bout me. Ah'm all right. *Ah've* ben *shot* beefo'!"

One by one the witnesses either by sight or by hearing were examined and cross-examined by me. Every foot of the ground of that fight and of the retreat was gone over by me, with others. I made notes as I examined. At the conclusion, I put aside as valueless every detail of which there was no corroborative testimony or evidence. The result was the story as I have told it. So I made my official report.

As the Germans gave their signal for retreat, they abandoned a considerable quantity of property, either in a spirit of panic, or in order to make themselves better prepared to carry the load of their dead and wounded. I cannot give off-hand the complete inventory; and, as I write, a copy of my report is not at hand. The abandoned property account included, however, the following items:

About 40 potato-masher grenades.

7 Long-arm wire cutters.

3 Caps (one of which was found in the state described above).

3 Lueger automatic pistols.

We found marks in the clay, outside the wire of the combat group, to show where two hospital corps stretchers had been set down during the fight.

From our knowledge that it was customary to equip no more than one man of every four with the heavy long-arm wire clipper we made the deduction that there were certainly no less than 24 men in that German patrol. The evidence of their having brought with them two stretchers was corroborative of such a deduction. Also, the fact that none of the dead or wounded were left in our hands, coupled with our knowledge that of the dead alone there were at least four, contributed convincingly to the conclusion that the enemy was of a minimum of 24 men.

And this attacking party was completely killed, wounded, or put to rout by one rather small of stature colored soldier, in civilian life a red-cap porter of the New York Central Railroad Station at Albany, N. Y.—by name, Henry Johnson.

By half past ten o'clock I had completed the examination and inspection of the witnesses and the scene of the fight, and dictated my official report, including the recommendation of both Johnson and Roberts for decorations of honor—for valor.

A few minutes later, an orderly reported that Colonel Hayward and three civilians were descending from the mule-car, just outside of my quarters. I hurried out to greet my visitors, and recognized Irvin Cobb, Martin Green of the *Evening World,* and Lincoln Eyre of the New York *World.*

Of course I just had to get those men out to Combat Group Number 29! It was a Heaven-sent opportunity for honorable publicity for our volunteer regiment from Harlem.

Cobb asked me if I could tell them of any interesting experience to include in the stories that they wanted to write of *"Les enfants perdu,"* whom they had just succeeded in finding after arduous and discouraging search.

I told them that things generally had been rather dull and quiet with us; but that amusing incidents, of course, were cropping up all the time.

"Have you had no fights, then?" chimed in Mr. Green.

"Why yes—we did have a little fight this morning, that was good while it lasted—if you're interested in that sort of thing," I answered. "Of course we get our shelling fairly constantly, and there's more or less sniping all the time; but, this morning a couple of our boys had a real pitched battle, for a few minutes. They did very well, too.

I've just finished the report. I'm trying to get them the *Croix de Guerre*. Would you care to read it?"

"Yes indeed!" The three journalists answered, all at once.

As they read, the only sounds in that little room were strange grunts and exhalations, emphasizing their appreciation of having dropped in upon one of the really sensational incidents of America's part in the war.

"You win, Little!" exclaimed Cobb, when the reading had been finished. "You played your hand well. How about our looking over the grounds—to get the picture right?"

"Delighted to take you out there!" I answered. "But you may get sniped at. If you don't mind that, let's go."

It was a very warm day. Cobb said:

"The sniping part's all right. A wound stripe would make me just irresistible; but how about taking my coat off?"

Three times on the way out, Cobb stopped short, as he mopped and panted, and swore that he wouldn't go another step. I felt sympathetic. The sun beat down mercilessly upon the shadeless plain. I did want those writers, however, to see that grenade-blown punch bowl filled with blood. I coaxed and encouraged. After four periods, the objective, Combat Group Number 29, was reached. I believe those journalists were actually satisfied with the reward of their physical effort, in the material for local color gained by their visit to that exposed post.

When we returned to my P.C., lunch was ready.

Towards the end of our luncheon, Cobb looked over at me and said:

"Little, I know it's against your rules to talk shop at table; but, today, just for one question, I want you to indulge me. How much special training for this trench fighting had that chap Henry Johnson had before he licked those 24 Germans?"

"Just the same as the rest of the regiment," I answered. "No more than three weeks in theory. As a matter of actual practice, taking out our time for changing stations, and the ordinary routine of our early days with the French, I should say that the special training of our men has been equal to about one week of what I understand the draft men are now getting at the big cantonments over home."

"Well," said Irvin Cobb, "I've been thinking. It seems to me that the performance of that young man was truly remarkable. Why, if he had had the normal training that our men at home are getting today, I believe that by tomorrow night Henry would have been storming Potsdam!"

A few days after the visit to our sector of Messrs. Cobb, Green, and Eyre, there appeared as a front page spread of the New York *World,* a signed article by the special staff correspondent, Lincoln Eyre, describing in detail "The Battle of Henry Johnson."

All the New York evening papers of that day carried quotations or reprints of the *World* beat. By the following morning the Associated Press had spread all over the United States the account of the prowess of America's first two colored soldiers to receive from the French Government the coveted *Croix de Guerre.* The 15th New York Infantry had passed out of the category of a merely unique organization of the American Army, a regiment with its chief bid for fame based upon the music of Jim Europe's Band.

Our colored volunteers from Harlem had become, in a day, one of the famous fighting regiments of the World War.

Upon February 17, 1919, Colonel Hayward saw his dream come true.

It may be recalled that during the early Summer of 1917, the 15th New York Infantry had suffered a number of disappointments which appeared to some almost in the light of slights.

For example: When the "Rainbow Division" was announced, with the 69th New York Infantry (which had not been included in the 27th Division) as one of the elements, Colonel Hayward had endeavored to get our regiment put in with the Rainbows, too—only to be informed, with a laugh, that black was not one of the colors of the rainbow. And when the 27th Division had staged a farewell parade, as the boys left New York to go into training at Spartanburg, once more the Fifteenth was left out of the day's program.

Our regiment had not been accorded the thrill of a going-away parade; and, within our ranks, there had been disappointment. Colonel Hayward had promised, in what to some had seemed to be a spirit of bitter recklessness, that we should have a parade when we should come home.

That promise had been worked to the limit within our regiment. The welcome home parade was a matter of daily discussion. After the armistice had been declared, the parade came to be a medium of disciplinary exactment. I believe there were nowhere in the whole army any better behaved soldiers than our soldiers. Our men had averaged well in deportment all through the war; but there were, of course, scapegraces in every company, just as in most families there are "black sheep." It was to the scapegraces that we addressed the threat of penalty of a deprivation of the privilege of parading with the regiment up Fifth Avenue, when the citizens of New York should turn out to welcome us home.

That threatened penalty had to be inflicted in but very few cases. In the majority of cases, the men just made up their minds not to miss that parade—and, accordingly, they carried on without delinquencies.

In the Spring of 1917, when the active recruiting effort was on, a parade had been attempted through the streets of Harlem, with a view of stirring the citizens to enthusiasm and prompting the youth of the colored race to enlist.

Someone had taken a photograph of that parade.

It was a dreadful picture to record. A couple of hundred men or less were shown in a stringy column of irregularity, which some wag had named, "Column of Bunches," and some other wag had added: "And not much of that."

The photograph had been shown to Colonel Hayward with a laugh and sneer.

The Colonel had taken a good, long look at that photograph. At first there had been red spots of anger in his cheeks. Then the cheeks had gone pale; and presently his eyes had closed. When Colonel Hayward had opened his eyes again the photograph upon which they had focussed was still there before them, but as the eyes rested upon the picture the second time, a new light and expression had come over the face of the man.

Then the boyish looking colonel had spoken: "Do you know," he had said to the officers who had been his companions, "Do you know, a kind of vision has come to me out of that picture—a dream, I suppose you might call it. And those poor little bunches of undisciplined looking soldiers have taken on a new and magnificent dignity. I'm looking a long ways ahead now, and I'm not sure whether I'm in the picture or not, but the men are there —only their numbers have increased twenty-fold. And the poor, dribbling column of bunches has become a splendid machine-like column of military strength. The spectators on the sidewalks have changed in appearance, too. There are more of them, and they seem to be greatly excited. Some are waving their hats, and apparently shouting. And some are crying, too. Some are smiling. But the ones who laugh, seem to be laughing with a different quality of laughter than the ones in this picture here today.

"Do you know," the Colonel mused on, "I'm having a kind of silly dream about that column of bunches. This visionary picture that I see shows the war to be ended, and these men marching home. And it's obvious that they've done well, too, and that their homecoming is one of triumph. I doubt if I ever shall forget that dream. I wonder if it can come true."

And within two years, upon February 17th, 1919, Colonel Hayward's dream did come true. The 15th New York Infantry, known in France as the 369th United States Infantry, marched up 5th Avenue to receive the plaudits of a million grateful citizens of New York, and then marched on for the full length of the Lenox Avenue Boulevard, through Harlem, to turn a quarter of a million of men, women, and children of the colored race wild with a frenzy of pride and joy and love.

We left Camp Upton at daybreak, ran by special trains into Long Island City, crossed the river upon ferry boats, marched through 35th Street to Madison Avenue, and down Madison Avenue until the head of the column rested upon 23rd Street. Thus far the parade had not started. The marching was by way of mobilization, by battalions, and in column of squads.

Upon Madison Avenue, as we extended north from 23rd Street, we formed phalanx by company. In the phalanx formation we marched with equalized companies of

16 squads each, 4 platoons of 4 squads each, in close line without interval—a solid mass of men about 35 feet square. The sergeants marched 2 paces in front of their platoons. Lieutenants marched on a line 3 paces in front of sergeants. The Captain marched 5 paces in front of the line of lieutenants. It was, I believe, the first time New York had witnessed such a formation for parade—a formation which we had learned from the French.

At about eleven o'clock in the morning word came that the city officials had passed up 5th Avenue on the way to the reviewing stand at 60th Street, and Colonel Hayward, for the last time gave to his regiment of colored volunteers, the order—*"Forward MARCH!"*

We marched west through 23rd Street, along the southern border of Madison Square Park, to 5th Avenue. At 5th Avenue we turned to the north. We were the first of the home-coming troops to march under the Victory Arch at 25th Street. We continued straight on to the north until we reached 110th Street. There we turned west to Lenox Avenue, and at Lenox Avenue we turned north again and paraded to 145th Street. At 145th Street we turned east to Lexington Avenue, where we boarded subway trains for downtown. At 33rd Street we detrained, and marched into the 71st Regiment Armory. There the citizens' committee had prepared a fine lunch (chicken, of course)—and an entertainment for all hands.

For the first time in the history of the regiment, the 15th New York Infantry as a whole had a roof over its head.

I doubt if any of us shall ever again be privileged to share in such thrills of varying emotions as were ours upon the 17th of February, 1919, thanks to the wholeheartedness of the citizens of New York.

New Yorkers are sometimes jeered at as a bustling,

hustling people so intent upon the pursuit and worship of the almighty dollar as to be lacking in spirits of hospitality, civic pride, and even patriotism. It is no part of my purpose, or present duty, to enter upon debate in refutation of such a slander.

New York's severest critics, however, could have found no fault with either the quantity or the quality of the red-blood which ruled the passions of its people that day upon which they welcomed home the 15th Heavy Foot.

I marched at the head of the 1st Battalion—about 60 paces (150 feet) behind Jim Europe's Band of sixty pieces of brass and reed, and a field music section of thirty trumpets and drums.

During the entire progress of that seven mile march, I scarcely heard ten consecutive bars of music. So great were the roars of cheers, the applause, and the shouts of personal greetings!

The multitude of fellow citizens who greeted us that day—the tens of thousands who cheered, the women who wept—the men who cried "God bless you, boys!"—all were united to drown the music of Jim Europe's Band. They did not give us their welcome because ours was a regiment of colored soldiers—they did not give us their welcome in spite of our being a regiment of colored soldiers. They greeted us that day from hearts filled with gratitude and with pride and with love, *because ours was a regiment of men, who had done the work of men.*

Upon the 17th of February, 1919, New York City knew no color line.

When we arrived at the Harlem districts, Colonel Hayward halted the regiment and ordered the formation changed.

That French phalanx formation of solid masses was impressive, and the parade in that formation was a great success down in that part of New York where the greetings were, for the most part, impersonal.

Up through the avenues of Harlem, however, such a formation would have been a cruelty. So far as might be possible, the face and figure of each soldier boy must be made to stand out, for his loved ones to see and to recognize.

We continued the march in platoon front, with good deep distances between front and rear ranks. And the music of Jim Europe's Band was—"Here comes my daddy now!"

And the new open formation proved itself as great a success for the home districts of the colored men as had the phalanx for Fifth Avenue.

Mothers, and wives, and sisters, and sweethearts recognized their boys and their men; and they rushed right out through the ranks to embrace them. For the final mile or more of our parade about every fourth soldier of the ranks had a girl upon his arm—and we marched through Harlem singing and laughing.

It may not have been good military business, but it was great human business. And a nation of great, honest, human emotion is a great nation.

11

FROM
Yes I Can
by Sammy Davis, Jr.
(1926–   )

When the Selective Service Act was passed in 1940 it was amended by a clause forbidding discrimination in the drafting and training of men. For some time, however, draft boards accepted only white men for training. Negroes began to protest loudly. In the fall of 1940 the War Department clarified its policy and issued a statement that Negroes would be received into the army on the general basis of the proportion of the Negro population of the country, but in segregated units. One million Negro men and women did serve in the armed forces during World War II, and this did represent the ratio that Negroes bore to the general population. Finally, in January, 1945, the War Department announced that Negro troops would be integrated with white troops in a unit to fight in Germany.

Military posts were the scene of innumerable clashes between black and white during the war. There were serious riots at Fort Bragg, Camp Robinson, Camp Davis, Camp Lee and Fort Dix.

When Sammy Davis entered the army, according to his autobiography, he did not have the protective shell necessary to ward off the blows of the racial hate that struck from all sides. Shielded by his father and uncle for the

early part of his life, Davis' army experience was his first
taste of the world as it really was. The racial strains were
doubly unfortunate in his case since he went into the
army thinking that being an American was the one "big
time" thing he had going for himself.

A PFC was sitting on the steps of a barracks, sewing an
emblem onto a shirt. I walked over to him. "Excuse me,
buddy. I'm a little lost. Can you tell me where 202 is?"

He jerked his head, indicating around the corner.
"Two buildings down. And I'm not your buddy, you
black bastard!" He turned back to his sewing.

The corporal standing outside 202 checked my name
against a list on a clipboard. "Yeah—well, you better wait
over there awhile 'til we figure out what to do with you."

I was at the Infantry's Basic Training Center at Fort
Francis E. Warren in Cheyenne, Wyoming.

I sat on the steps where he'd pointed. Other guys were
showing up and he checked them off his list and told
them, "Go inside and take the first bunk you see." I
looked away for a moment and heard him saying, "Sit
over there with Davis."

A tall, powerfully built guy dropped his gear alongside
mine. "My name's Edward Robbins." We shook hands
and he sat down next to me. One by one, men were arriving and being sent inside. They kept on coming but
no one else was told to wait with us. Then, finally, there
was no point in hoping against the obvious. It was clear
that we were the only ones being held outside while all
the white guys were going right in.

The corporal went inside. We were sitting in front of
a screen door so even though he lowered his voice I could
hear every word he was saying. " . . . look, we got a

problem. Those niggers out there are assigned to this company. I'm gonna stick 'em down there. You two guys move your gear so I can give 'em those last two bunks."

Another voice said, "Hey, that's right nexta me. I ain't sleepin' near no dingo."

"Look, soldier, let's get something straight right off. I'm in charge of this barracks and . . ."

"I ain't arguin' you're in charge. I'm only sayin' I didn't join no nigger army."

Embarrassed in front of each other, Edward and I looked straight ahead.

". . . what about the can? Y'mean we gotta use the same toilets as them?"

"That's right, soldier. They use the same latrine we all use. Now look, we got no goddamned choice. They used t'keep 'em all together, but now for some goddamned reason they sent 'em here and we just gotta put up with 'em. . . ."

It was impossible to believe they were talking about me.

"Yeah, but I still ain't sleepin' nexta no nigger."

"What the hell's the army need 'em for? They'll steal ya blind while ya sleep and there ain't one of 'em has any guts. They're all yeller bellies. . . ."

"Awright, knock it off. I don't want 'em any more than you do but we're stuck with 'em. That's orders."

They weren't even trying to keep their voices down any more.

There was the sound of iron beds sliding across the wooden floor. The corporal beckoned from the doorway. "Okay, c'mon in and I'll assign you your bunks. Let's go," he snapped, "on the double." We picked up our gear and followed him through the door. I felt like a disease he was bringing in.

There were rows of cots on both sides with an aisle down the center. The guys were standing in groups. They'd stopped talking. I looked straight ahead. I could feel them staring as we followed the corporal down the aisle. He pointed to the last two cots on one side. "These are yours. Now, we don't want no trouble with you. Keep your noses clean, do as you're told, and we'll get along." He walked away.

I looked around the barracks. The bed nearest to ours was empty. All the cots were about two feet apart from each other except ours, which were separated from the rest by about six feet—like we were on an island.

A few of the men sort of smiled and half-waved hello. Some wouldn't look over at us. The nearest, a tall, husky guy who must have been a laborer or an athlete, kept his back turned.

A sergeant came in and from the center of the barracks announced, "I'm Sergeant Williams. I'm in charge of this company and I. . . ." His glance fell on the space between the beds. He turned to the corporal. "What the hell is that?"

The corporal quietly explained how he'd handled things. Sergeant Williams listened, then spoke sharply: "There is only one way we do things here and that's the Army way! There will be exactly three feet of space, to the inch, between every bed in this barracks. You have sixty seconds to replace the beds as you found them. *Move!*"

He came over to me. "What's your name, soldier?"

"Sammy Davis, Jr."

"Of all the men in this barracks did you arrive first or tenth or last or what?"

"About in the middle."

"Did you choose this bunk?"

"Well, no, I was told. . . ."

He looked around. By this time the barracks had been rearranged. "All right, Davis. Move your gear one bunk over." He turned to Edward. "You do the same."

He addressed us all. "No man here is better than the next man unless he's got the rank to prove it."

I sat on the end of my bunk, the shock gone, immense anger growing within me until my legs were shaking and it was impossible for me to keep them still. I couldn't give them the satisfaction of seeing how they'd gotten to me. I saw one of the other guys polishing his boots. That was a good idea. The boots were a brand new, almost yellow leather and we'd been told to darken them with polish. I took off my watch and laid it carefully on the bed. I opened my shoe shine kit, took out the polish and brush, and began rubbing the polish into the leather, doing the same spot over and over, concentrating on it, working so hard that I could blank out everything else from my mind. Suddenly another pair of boots landed at my feet. "Here, boy, you can do mine, too."

I looked up. It was the guy who had the bed next to me, and he'd already turned away. I grabbed for the boots, to throw them at his head—but I didn't want to make trouble, not on my first day in camp. I put them down beside his bed.

He looked at me, surprised. "Hey, boy, don't get me wrong, I expected t'give you a tip. Maybe two-bits for a good job."

"I'm no bootblack. And I'm no boy, either."

"Whoa now, don't get so uppity, boy. Hell, if you don't wanta make the money it's okay by me." He shrugged and walked over to Edward. "Here y'are, boy. You can do 'em."

"Yes, suh. Glad t'do 'em, suh."

"Well, that's more like it. Glad somebody around here knows his place. And you don't have to call me sir. Just call me Mr. Jennings. Y'see in the Army you only call the officers 'sir.' "

"Yes, suh, Mr. Jennings and my name is Edward. Anything you needs. . . ."

I wanted to vomit. I was alone in that barracks.

Jennings was talking to a couple of the other guys. "This may work out okay. One of 'em's not a half-bad nigger." He came by Edward's bunk with three more pairs of boots. Edward's face fell for a second but he brightened up right away. "Yes, suh, you just leave 'em here and I'll take care of 'em."

"You oughta thank me for settin' up this nice little business for you."

"I *do* thank you." He smiled broadly. "Oh, yes suh. I thanks you kindly."

Edward was avoiding my eyes. Eventually he looked up and moved his head just the slightest bit. For a split second he opened up to me and I saw the humiliation he was enduring because his fear of trouble was stronger than his need for dignity. I hoped he'd look up again so I could let him know I was sorry I'd judged him and forced him to let me look inside him and see the pain and weakness that was his right to hide.

Perhaps this was how he had to live, but I wasn't going to take it from anybody. I wasn't going to let anybody goad me into fights and get myself in trouble, either. I was going to mind my own business and have a clean record.

Jennings flopped onto his bunk. He sat up, reached over and took my watch off my bed. "Say, this ain't a half-bad watch." He looked at me suspiciously.

"Put it back."

"Hold on, now. My, but you're an uppity one." He stood up. "Hey, Philips . . . catch!" He tossed the watch across the barracks. I ran to get it back but just as I reached Philips he lobbed it over my head to another guy who threw it back to Jennings. I ran after it, knowing how ridiculous I looked getting there just as Jennings threw it over my head again, that I shouldn't chase after it, that I was only encouraging them, but I was afraid they'd drop it and I couldn't stop myself.

"Atten*shun*!!!" Every head in the barracks snapped toward the doorway. Sergeant Williams walked straight to Jennings. "What've you got there?"

Jennings opened his hand and showed him my watch. "Whose is it?"

Jennings shrugged.

"It's mine."

Sergeant Williams brought it to me. Jennings grinned. "Hell, Sarge, we were just kiddin' around. I was only showing the watch to the guys."

"You're a wise guy, Jennings. In the Army we respect another man's property. You just drew K.P. for a week." He left the barracks.

Jennings looked at me with more hatred than I had ever seen on a man's face. "You just wait. I'll fix you for this, black boy."

Hours after lights-out I lay awake trying to understand. How many white people had felt like this about me? I couldn't remember any. Not one. Had I just been too stupid to see it? I thought of the people we'd known—agents, managers, the acts we'd worked with—these people had all been friends. I know they were. There were so many things I had to remember: the dressing rooms—had we been stuck at the end of corridors off by ourselves? Or with the other colored acts? That was ridiculous. Dressing rooms were always assigned according to our spot on the bill. And the places we stayed? They *were* almost always colored hotels and rooming houses, but I'd never thought of them like that. They were just *our* rooming houses. But, did we *have* to go to them? Didn't we just go to them because they knew us and because they were the cheapest? Or wasn't that the reason? Sure there were people who hadn't liked us, but it had always been "Don't pay attention, Poppa, he's just jealous 'cause we got a better act." Or, "They don't like us 'cause we're in show business." And I'd never questioned it. In the last few years I'd known there was prejudice and hate in the world. I remembered several times Will telling me, "Someday you'll understand." But I didn't understand and I couldn't believe I ever would.

The physical grind of basic training wasn't as rough on me as on some of the others because as a dancer I was in good shape. I didn't mind the food. I'd had far worse and far less.

Most of the men in our barracks gave me no problems, either because they didn't care, or because after a day of Basic they were too tired to worry what the hell I was. But there were about a dozen I had to look out for. They clustered around Jennings and their unity alone was enough to intimidate anybody who might have wanted to show friendliness toward me. When that group wasn't around, the others would be pleasant, but as soon as one of them showed up, it was as if nobody knew me. The sneers, the loud whispers, the hate-filled looks were bad enough, but I didn't want it to get worse. I tried to keep peace with Jennings without Tom-ing him as Edward was doing. I hoped that if I was good at my job he'd respect me, but when I was good on the rifle range he hated me all the more. If I was bad he laughed at me. I found myself walking on eggs to stay out of his way, casually but deliberately standing on a different chow line, always finding a place at one end of the tables far away from him in the mess hall.

I was dressing, fastening the strap on my watch before evening mess and it slipped off my wrist and fell to the floor next to Jennings' bed. Before I could reach it he stood up and ground it into the floor with the heel of his boot. I heard the crack. He lifted his foot, smiling coyly, "Oh! What *have* I gone and done? Sure was foolish of you to leave your watch on the floor. Too bad, boy. Tough luck."

The glass was crushed and the gold was twisted. The winding stem and the hands were broken off and mangled. I put the pieces on the bed and looked at them, foolishly trying to put them together again.

"Awww, don't carry on, boy. You can always steal another one."

I looked at him. "What've you got against me?"

"Hell, I ain't got nothin' against you, boy. I like you fine."

I knew I shouldn't just take it from him like this. I knew I should swing at him or something, but I was so weakened from the hurt of it that I couldn't get up the anger.

I wrapped the pieces in some paper and put it in my pocket. Maybe it could still be fixed.

Overnight the world looked different. It wasn't one color any more. I could see the protection I'd gotten all my life from my father and Will. Yet, I couldn't thank them for it. I appreciated their loving hope that I'd never need to know about prejudice and hate, but they were wrong. It was as if I'd walked through a swinging door for eighteen years, a door which they had always secretly held open. But they weren't there to hold it open now, and when it finally hit me it was worse than if I'd learned about it gradually and knew how to move with it.

Sergeant Williams walked out of the mess hall with me. "I was looking over the service records and I see that you were in show business. We have shows at the service club every Friday. If you'd care to help out I'm sure it would be appreciated, and perhaps you might enjoy doing it."

After the show, I was standing backstage with one of the musicians, a guy from another company, and I suggested we go out front and have a coke.

He said, "Maybe we better go over to the colored service club. You don't want trouble, do you?"

"Trouble? I just entertained them for an hour. They cheered me. Hey, look, God knows I don't want trouble but there's gotta be a point where you draw the line. Now I don't know about you, but I'm thirsty and I'm goin' in for a coke."

A few of the guys who'd seen the show saw us walking in and pulled chairs up to their tables, making room for us. Jennings was at a table with four of his buddies. They looked over at me and smiled or smirked, I couldn't be sure which. I sat with a group from our barracks and it was the happiest hour I'd spent in the Army. I luxuriated in it. I had earned their respect; they were offering their friendship and I was grabbing for it.

After an hour or so I said good night and headed for the door. As I passed Jennings' table he stood up. "Hey, Davis, c'mon over here and let's get acquainted." He was smiling, holding out his hand. It would have been satisfying to brush him off, but if he was trying to be friendly it seemed better to accept it and keep peace. "Well, I was going back to the barracks. . . ."

"Hell, you got time for one little drink with us." He pulled out a chair for me. "Man, where'd you learn t' dance like that? I swear I never saw a man's feet move so fast. By the way, you notice I ain't callin' you 'boy.' "

"Have a beer, Davis." One of the guys pushed a bottle toward me. "Here y' are," Jennings said, "here's one no-body touched."

"If you don't mind I'd rather have a coke."

"Hey, old buddy, you're in the army. It's time you got over that kid stuff. You gotta learn to drink like a man. Try it. You're gonna like it."

The others were watching me. One of them grinned. "Yeah, you oughta learn to drink if you're gonna be a soldier."

Jennings said, "Listen, you're gonna insult me in a minute. Any man who won't drink with me. . . ."

"Okay, I'll try it."

"That's better. Now I'll tell you how to drink beer. It can't be sipped like whiskey or a coke. To really get the taste of beer you've gotta take a good long slug."

The others nodded and raised their bottles. Jennings said, "Here's to you." I picked up my bottle to return their toast. I had it halfway to my mouth when I realized it wasn't cold. It was warm. As it came close to my nose I got a good whiff of it. It wasn't beer.

"Hell, don't smell it, man! Drink it!"

I took another smell and all at once I understood the smiles, the handshakes, the friendliness from Jennings. Somebody had taken the bottle empty into the men's room and came back with it filled.

Jennings was saying, "Come on, drink up, boy. . . ."

I put the bottle on the table. The faces in front of me

zoomed in like a movie close-up and I could see every line, every bead of perspiration, every blink of their eyes. The noise in the room was growing loud then low, loud then low. Suddenly I snapped out of it.

"Drink it yourself, you dirty louse."

Jennings roared with laughter. "Hell, he even curses like a coke drinker, don't he?"

I tried to stand up but my chair wouldn't move. Jennings had his foot behind a leg of it, trapping me. The old hate was back in his face. "You wanta live with us and you wanta eat with us and now you came in here and you wanta drink with us. I kinda thought you loved us so much you'd wanta. . . ."

I felt a warm wetness creeping over the side of my shirt and pants. While he'd been talking he had turned the bottle upside down and let it run out on me. I stared at the dark stain spreading over the khaki cloth, stared at it in unbelieving horror, cringing from it, trying to lean away from my wet shirt and wet pants. My pocket was so soaked I couldn't put my hand in for my handkerchief.

Jennings jumped up, pointing to me, peering loudly. "Silly niggers can't even control themselves. This little fella got so excited sittin' with white men—look what he did to himself."

I was out of the chair and on top of him. I had my hands on his throat with every intention of killing him. I loved seeing the sneer fall from his face and be replaced by dumb shock as I squeezed tighter and tighter, my thumbs against his windpipe. He was gasping for breath. In a desperate effort he swung around fast, lifting me off the floor. My own weight dragged me off him and I flew through the air and crashed into one of the tables. Within seconds the area was cleared as though we were in a ring together.

Until this moment it hadn't been a fight, it had been an attack by 115 pounds of rage propelled by blind impulse. I hadn't known it was going to happen any more than Jennings had. The weeks of taking it, the time of looking for peace, of avoiding trouble, had simply passed, and it just happened, like a pitcher overflows when you put too much into it.

But we both knew it was going to be different now; he was a foot taller than me and half again my weight, or more, and without the advantage of surprise I was like a toy to him. He was taking his time, grinning to his friends, caressing the knuckles of one hand with the palm of the other. He raised his fists and began circling, licking his lips, anticipating the pleasure he was going to take out of me.

I flew into him with every bit of strength I had. His fist smashed into my face. Then I just stood there watching his other fist come at me, helpless to make myself move out of the way. I felt my nose crumble as if he'd hit an apple with a sledge hammer. The blood spurted out and I smelled a dry, horrible dusty smell.

"Get up, you yellow-livered black bastard, you stinking coon nigger. . . ." I hadn't realized I was on the floor. I got to my feet and stumbled toward him. He hit me in the stomach and I collapsed. I was gasping for breath but no air was coming in and I was suffocating. Then suddenly I could taste air, and the figures in front of my eyes straightened out and became people again. I got up and went for him. He was methodically hitting me over and over again, landing four to every one of my punches, but they weren't hurting me any more, they were just dull thuds against my body. Then his fist was beating down on the top of my head like a club. Someone shouted, "Don't hit 'em on the head, Jen. Y' can't hurt a nigger 'cept below the forehead." He kept pounding me and I felt myself slipping to the floor again. I grabbed his shirt with one hand to keep myself from falling so I could hit him in the face with my other hand. I had to stay on my feet and keep hitting him, nothing else mattered, and I was glad to trade being hit ten times by him for the joy of feeling my fist smash into his face just once. I hung on and kept hitting him and hitting and hitting. . . .

A guy named O'Brien, from my barracks, was holding a wet cloth against my face. "You'll be okay," he said. "The bleeding's stopped."

We were outside. I was propped up against the side of the PX. It was very quiet. Another guy was there. Miller. They were part of the group that always avoided trouble with Jennings. He smiled. "You might feel better to know that you got in your licks. I think you closed one of his eyes and you definitely broke his nose. He's wearing it around his left ear." I started to laugh but a shock of pain seared my lips. My head was pounding like it was still being hit. I opened my mouth carefully to ask how long I'd been out.

O'Brien said, "Take it easy." He grinned and showed me the cloth he was wiping my face with. "You ripped his shirt when you fell and you had part of it in your hands. You had a death grip on it even after you went out."

They walked me back to the barracks. Sergeant Williams was waiting in the doorway. He shook his head in disgust. "Very smart! Well, get over to the infirmary with Jennings." He walked into his bedroom.

I had sent Jennings to the infirmary. What beautiful news. Gorgeous! Miller and O'Brien were waiting to take me there. I shook my head and thanked them. I wasn't going to give Jennings the satisfaction of seeing me in the infirmary, not if my nose fell off entirely.

Lights were out but on the way to my bunk some of the guys stopped me and told me that when I'd fallen off Jennings he was starting to stomp me but Miller and O'Brien had stepped in and pulled him away. I realized that I'd broken the barracks into two groups: the haters, and the guys in the middle who didn't care enough to take sides or who didn't want to get involved. It had never occurred to me that some might swing over to my side. But when Miller and O'Brien saw that I was down and Jennings was *still* kicking me they had to get involved, and say, "Hey, wait a minute. This is ridiculous. Nobody's *that* bad."

I got into bed and it was delicious. I tried to turn over on my stomach but the bruises were murder. Still, as much as I hurt, as awful as it had been, the worst pain wasn't so bad that I wouldn't do it again for the dignity I got from hitting back.

Jennings had beaten me unconscious and hurt me more than I'd hurt him, but I had won. He was saying, "God made me better than you," but lost the argument the minute he had to use his fists to prove it. All he'd proven is that he was physically stronger than me, but that's not what we were fighting over.

I'd never been so tired in my life, but I couldn't sleep. I hated myself for those weeks of sneaking around trying to avoid trouble. I'd been insane to imagine there was anything I could do to make a Jennings like me. I hadn't begun to understand the scope of their hatred. I was haunted by that voice yelling, "Y' can't hurt 'em 'cept below the forehead." My God, if they can believe that then they don't even know what I am. The difference they see is so much more than color. I'm a whole other brand of being to them.

There was so much to think about. How long would I have gone on not knowing the world was made up of haters, guys in the middle, Uncle Toms . . . I couldn't believe I was going to spend the rest of my life fighting with people who hate me when they don't even know me. But I kept hearing that voice and I knew I'd hear it again, out of another mouth, from another face, but spouting the same ignorance. I tried to stay awake to think it out, but my head was throbbing and the room began tilting to the left, then the right. . . .

12

FROM
A Choice of Weapons
by Gordon Parks
(1912–   )

*One would have thought that by the time World War II
started, discrimination in the armed forces would have
been a thing of the past. Unfortunately, racial unrest
abounded, and the irony of black men giving their lives
for a country which denied them equality and basic rights
became even more painfully obvious than it had been in
the past.*

*Gordon Parks was brought up in a small town in Kan-
sas in the early 1900s. He worked at a succession of temporary jobs—piano player, bellhop, waiter—until he began his career as a photographer. Parks has been a staff
photographer for* Life *since 1949. He is also a writer
and composer whose music has been performed in major
cities.*

*In the following selection he recounts his bitter expe-
riences as a press corps member assigned to an air force
unit during the war.*

The hot air smelled of gasoline and planes when I arrived
at Selfridge Field the next morning. Though it was early
the sprawling air base was alive with men and all kinds
of machines, from jeeps to P-40 fighter ships. A sergeant
met me at the gate in a command car; and, as we halted

at company headquarters, a squadron of fighter ships thundered up into the hot sky. I stood marveling at the climbing ships, finding pleasure in the fact that black boys were inside them. And, thinking back to Richard Wright's *Native Son*, I recalled the Negro boy's remark when he witnessed a similar sight: "Look at those white boys fly," he had said in a special sort of awe. Now I was thinking the same thing about these black boys as they flashed above the earth like giant birds.

"That's Wild Bill Walker's squadron taking off," the sergeant said admiringly. "He's one of our best pilots."

Colonel Davis greeted me with a firm handshake that is indispensable to West Point men. He was straight, tall and light brown. His boyish face belied the self-restraint that lay underneath. The son of Benjamin Davis, Sr., the first Negro general, he took his soldiering seriously. He had just returned from overseas, where he had led the 99th Fighter Squadron into combat. "He goes by the book," one of his officers was to tell me later. "The *Army Manual* is his bible and God help those who disobey it."

We talked for about a half hour; and I am afraid neither of us got much from the meeting. He was neither friendly nor distant, just austere. He asked me orderly questions and I gave him orderly answers; and I left him feeling that he was not a man given to warm friendship. And, in his business, he was probably better off for it, I thought.

The pilots seemed to be a contented group of men. They were at last doing what they had fought so hard to do—fly. They were the best to be picked from the colleges around the country; and there were some excellent pilots among them. The ground officers and their crews were also of the highest caliber. It had the makings of a first-rate fighter group.

I had known the armament officer, Hank Bowman,

from Minnesota, remembering him as a gangly kid who used to flip newspapers sideways from his bike as he rode along. He and Tony Weaver, a ground officer on Colonel Davis's staff, soon became my closest friends. And almost immediately they insisted that I discard my civilian clothes and get into my correspondent's uniform. I had wanted to keep it fresh for overseas; but when I awoke the third morning my civvies had disappeared. My officer's cap had been wet down the night before and stuck under my mattress. It now looked as if it had flown a hundred missions. Hank and Tony only smiled when I inquired about my other clothes. I would either have to wear the uniform or go about the base naked. I chose the uniform.

I slept in the barracks with the officers and I ate with them. On the fourth day Colonel Davis granted my flying privileges. Certain pilots were assigned to fly me along on the simulated missions. Most of the time it was Captain George Knox. At other times it was either Gleed, Wild Bill Walker or Wendell Pruitt—all fine pilots and fine men.

Now my days took on an entirely new meaning. I would tumble out of bed at six each morning, shower, eat, jump into my flying suit and hurry to the flight line loaded down with my cameras and notebooks.

There is something about a flying field that makes a heart beat faster; the acrid odor of the petrol has its own way of stimulating the senses, the motors roaring for take-off, the familiar parrotlike voice of the control tower talking you into position, the barreling down the runway and the final liftoff, the circling for echelon positions; plane *two* comes up and takes position—plane *three*—plane *four*—plane *five,* then *six.* You look across the sky at four o'clock and they are all lined up beside you, men and machines roaring through the upper reaches.

When the bad weather came in, we sat about the ready huts telling jokes and playing blackjack or poker, sniffing now and then at the sky; then, when the clouds lifted enough for takeoff, we would hurry to the ships and fly until chow time. On one such day several of us were gathered in the weather shack when we heard a plane overhead. "Who in hell could be up there in soup like that?" someone said. And we all stopped talking to listen in on the intercom to the tower.

"Redbird to tower—redbird to tower. I'm floundering—bring me in. Over."

"But we're socked in here, redbird. Try to make it to Oscoda. Over."

"Fuel's too low. I've got to come in here. Give me a bearing. Over."

"You're too high and too far north, redbird. Circle sixty degrees left and start letting down slowly. Over. Come in, redbird. Over."

"It's Jimmy Higgins," someone said. "Where in hell is he coming from?" No one answered.

"Come in, redbird. This is the tower. Over."

Silence.

"Come in, redbird. Do you hear me, redbird? This is the tower. Come in, redbird. Over."

Now a distant whining pierced the damp morning. I glanced at the other pilots. But they were all staring tensely at the floor.

"Redbird—come in. Redbird, this is the tower. Come in. Over!"

The whining was growing louder. We all knew now. He was spinning in. "Get out, Jimmy," someone pleaded softly.

"Redbird, redbird, this is the tower. Are you in trouble?"

The whine was nearing the earth now and after a split second we heard the crash. When we reached the spot several minutes later, there was only a gaping twenty-foot hole filled with twisted metal. A smell of petrol and fresh earth filled our nostrils and we stood helpless on the rim of the hole watching little columns of steam and smoke rise from the rutted earth. Somewhere down in that snarled darkness was Jimmy Higgins.

After such a thing had happened, everyone flew again as soon as possible. It was not good to let fear set in. So no sooner had the clouds rolled back than the squadrons of the 332nd began taking off, flying tighter than ever, diving even more recklessly at the gunnery targets, hedge-hopping over trees and executing breath-taking slow rolls. That same afternoon George Knox and I were lumbering along in a trainer toward Oscoda, Michigan. Only the droning motor broke the silence over the peaceful countryside. Far beneath us I could see cows grazing, a tractor crawling over a thin slice of black earth. Now and then we would knife through a patch of white cloud, then we were in the clear blue again; and I began to wonder about Jimmy Higgins falling through space that morning. What was it like to be trapped in a capsule of metal and steel, hurtling toward earth and death? Did he close his eyes and await the impact, or did he die trying to pull out of the spin, hoping for a miracle that never came? Suddenly we were in the midst of a roar; I thought our plane was shaking to pieces. My heart sank and fear shot through my body. But, before I could react further, six P-40's zoomed up and away from us in spiraling bursts of speed.

"You crazy bastards!" George was hollering over the radio. "I'll have every damned one of you court-martialed!" Then he looked around at me and laughed.

"Got any toilet paper, George?" I asked.

"That's Bright and his bunch of clowns. That's what they call giving you a tweeker."

"Well, I'm still tweeking!" I called back. George pointed down to our left. "Look," he said. The planes had regrouped and they were hopping over trees, barns and farmhouses. Chickens were flying through the air. Cows were running along the pasture in fright. George knew, and I knew; it was all a crazy tribute to Higgins.

We spent our weekends in Detroit. And Paradise Valley, a Negro section of the city, opened its arms wide to the nattily uniformed pilots and officers. They were already heroes to these people who had never seen black boys with wings on their chests before. There was no shortage of women; they came from miles around—"in furs, Fords and Cadillacs," Tony used to crow in delight. The problem was to pick wisely from the multitude. Tony was cocky, proud and brazen with good humor; and he was like a one-eyed dog in a sausage factory after two weeks at the base. A very unpretty woman approached him one night at a bar, but Tony, his sights fixed on something more choice, ignored her. Hours later, when we were leaving the bar loaded and broke, the woman passed us and got into a beautiful new Cadillac. Tony stopped in his tracks. Then, walking up to the woman, he tipped his hat, "Baby," he said, "you look like King Kong, but this car and those furs you've got on are a natural gas. Move over, honey. Let Tony baby drive this thing back to camp." She smiled, moved over and we journeyed out to Selfridge in style.

As the training went into fall, the men's attitude began to change. The fun was about over now. And the talk of women and the joking gave way to more serious things. Racial tensions began to have an effect on their actions and thinking. There were several incidents of white enlisted men on the base not saluting Negro officers. And black soldiers in combat were writing back about being segregated in barracks and mess halls in the war zones. The Negro newspapers were filled with stories about the black men being turned from the factory gates when war plants cried desperately for more help. The Pittsburgh *Courier* carried a long piece about Negro soldiers being assigned to menial labor. And there was a front-page article about an army band playing "God Bless America" when the white soldiers boarded the troopships; then, when Negroes went up the gangplank, the band switched to "The Darktown Strutters' Ball."

And one Sunday night a race riot erupted in Detroit. Fighting spread all over the city; twenty-five Negroes and nine whites were killed and hundreds of both races were injured. The black man was beginning to meet humiliation with violence. White supremacy had become as much an enemy as "blood" and "race" doctrines of the Nazis. Vindictiveness was slowly spreading through the air base. One could feel it in the air, in the mess halls, the barracks and the ready huts.

Once, after I returned from a trip to Washington, I found a note Tony had left for me. It read:

Dear Gordon,
   Sorry to miss you but I'm on my way to Steubenville with Judy Edwards' body. As you probably heard, poor Judy spun in and I had to take his body all the way to Detroit because "there are no facilities" for handling Negro dead up there at Oscoda. It's about three hundred miles from Oscoda to Detroit, and in a goddamn Army ambulance you can imagine how long it took us to get there. Even as I

write this to you, my feelings keep swinging from a murderous rage to frustration. How could anybody do anything like this?

His body was lying wrapped in a tarpaulin in the back of the ambulance; and I had trouble accepting the fact that he was dead, for every time I looked back there, the body seemed to move. I now wonder if the doctors at the hospital had examined him, since this would have required them to touch him too. By the time night had fallen I felt so badly that all I could say was "Judy, I'm sorry. . . . I'm sorry. . . ." We have all suffered some brutal indignities from the whites in this country but this was the final indignity of all. All during the trip I was in an emotional state, alternately talking to the driver and quietly crying for Judy, for his family, for the country and for myself. I felt shame and revulsion for having to wear the uniform I had on. The driver seemed to be caught up in the same mood. We were two of the loneliest soldiers in the world.

I won't tell his folks about this trip because it will just hurt them more. At least to them he was a hero and I'll make sure that when I arrive in Steubenville everyone knows it. The whole dirty business will come into even sharper focus when they lower him into the grave. He'll get an honor guard (a white one), the rifle fire and all the trappings. See you when I get back.

Tony

I stuffed the letter into my pocket and walked over to the airstrip. The night was clear and cold and the stars seemed lower than usual. The fighter ships lined up on the quiet field were ghostly. I walked along beside them, noted the names stenciled in white block letters on the cockpits: Gleed, Pruitt, Tresville, Knox, Bright, Walker and many others. How many of these names will be on little white crosses this time next year? I wondered. At least the 332nd would go into battle with pilots who had faced the enemy before. This would be more of a chance than the 99th Squadron was allowed; for, unlike the white pilots, they had gone into their first battle without one seasoned pilot to lead them. The costly pattern of segregation had arranged a lonely death for some of these men—even over enemy territory. Hitler's Luftwaffe must have laughed when they screamed into the formations of those *schwarz* boys—knowing there wasn't an experienced fighter amongst them.

The next morning Wild Bill Walker, Hank and I ate breakfast together. It was a sparkling day, and we looked forward to some good flying hours. Wild Bill was supposed to have flown me that morning but at the last minute he had been assigned to a trainee from Tuskegee. He was to teach him echelon maneuvers. "Just my luck," he said, "when the gang'll probably be hot riding up to Oscoda." Pruitt flew me instead. And we went up to about fifteen thousand feet waiting for the others to join the formation. Above us and far to our right we could see Wild Bill taking the trainee through the various turns. "That's a hairy job with new men," Pruitt said over the intercom. We continued to circle, keeping the two planes in sight. Then the unbelievable thing was happening right before our eyes. The trainee's propeller was chewing up Wild Bill's tail. Then came the awful sight of the two broken ships plummeting and spinning toward earth. Pruitt gasped, "They're gone. Poor Bill's gone." He banked steeply and passed over the ships just as they hit the earth; then he called the tower. "Bluebird to tower—

bluebird to tower. We're coming in—it's awful—over."

"Come in, bluebird. Come in, bluebird," came the answer. There was sadness in the voice from the tower.

A little after mid-December an order came from the Pentagon halting all furloughs. We knew what this meant. Any day now we would be going overseas. A new tempo hit the base; the men rushed about, restless, patting one another's backs, awaiting moving orders. They came one morning about a week before Christmas. That afternoon Colonel Davis called me to headquarters. "We're about to pull out," he said, "and your traveling papers are not in order."

"What's wrong with them?" I asked.

"You'll have to take that up with Washington. I'd advise you to fly there. We'll probably be leaving before they can get word back here to you."

I packed the battle gear that had been issued to me that morning, took a bus to Detroit, then a plane to Washington; I arrived there late that evening. Stryker had left the OWI by now and had gone to work in New York for the Standard Oil Co. In fact, just about everyone I knew there had gone; the rest were preparing to leave. Besides, it was a weekend and no officials were around. I didn't know where to turn. The one man I did reach had developed a strange case of laryngitis, and was unable to talk, he said. Finally in desperation I tried to reach Elmer Davis, head of the OWI, but he was away on a trip. I fretted through Saturday and Sunday. Then the first thing Monday morning I went to see Ted Poston, a friend of mine in the OWI press section. He had heard the rumors. And Ted put things in their true perspective: "There's some Southern gentlemen and conservative Republicans on Capitol Hill who don't like the idea of giving this kind of publicity to Negro soldiers."

I was shocked—and so was Ted—but there wasn't much we could do about it. The next day I reached Elmer Davis by telephone and told him my story. He listened attentively. When I finished he said, "Don't worry, Gordon, I'll be in touch with the Pentagon this afternoon. You report there tomorrow. I'm sure everything will be all right."

That night, on the Howard University campus, I met Captain Lee Rayford and Lieutenant Walter Lawson, two pilots from the 99th Fighter Squadron. They had returned to the States after completing their required number of missions. Captain Rayford was the holder of the Purple Heart, the Distinguished Flying Cross, the Croix de Guerre, the Air Medal, and the Yugoslav Red Star. He had been shot up over Austria by a Messerschmitt 109. Both of them could have remained Stateside as instructors. Instead they had volunteered to go back to the war zone. We ate dinner together, and since they had to go to the Pentagon the next day we agreed to meet and go together.

We had no sooner boarded the bus and seated ourselves behind the driver than his voice came at us, metallic and demanding. "If you fellas wanta ride into Virginyuh, you gotta go to the rear." We looked at one another questioningly, deciding in our silence not to move. The driver stood up and faced us, a scrawny disheveled man with tobacco-stained teeth and a hawk nose. The armpits of his uniform were discolored from sweat. "You all heard what I said. This bus ain't goin' nowhere till you all go to the back where you belong."

"We intend going to Virginia in the seats we're in," Lee said with finality.

"Okay, if you ain't back there in one minute I'm callin' the MP's and havin' you put off."

"You'd better start calling right now," Lee replied.

Two white Air Force captains and a major were seated across the aisle from us and I noticed that they stirred uncomfortably. Several other whites were scattered in the near-empty bus and an elderly Negro woman sat at the rear. I watched her through the rear-view mirror. She had half risen from her seat; there was courage, dignity and anger in every line of her small body. Her look demanded that we stay there, and I was determined not to disappoint her. The bus had become dead quiet while the driver stood glowering at us.

"Fellows." One of the young white captains was speaking now. "We know how you feel about this," he said, his voice cloaked in false camaraderie, "but the major has an appointment at the Pentagon in a half hour. He wonders if you would mind moving back so that we can be on our way?"

My two friends were outranked. But there were no bars on my shoulders. The American eagle on my officer's cap was as large and significant as his or the major's. I took a good look at the old woman in the rear. She was standing now, gripping the seat ahead of her. Then, borrowing the captain's icy politeness, I stood and addressed the major. "Sir," I said, "as you can see, these men are fighter pilots. They have completed their missions but they have volunteered for more duty at the front. Would you like to order your fellow officers to the rear? They have no intention of moving otherwise." My anger was rising, so I sat back down.

The bus driver stood watching us until the major finally spoke to him. "Drive on," he said. "Can't you tell when you're licked?" The driver cursed under his breath, threw himself into the seat and slammed in the gears and we lurched off toward Virginia. "Hallelujah!" the Negro woman shouted from the rear. "Hallelujah!" Her voice rang with pathos and triumph. "Thank God we don't have to sit in the back of our P-38's," Lawson sighed as we got off the bus.

The three of us parted soon after. "We'll see you on the other side of somewhere," Rayford said cheerfully. And I watched the two young men walk away from me at the entrance to the Pentagon, hoping that I would meet up with them again. Our thoughts were already separated from the incident on the bus. We had won; our anger was dead.

The officer in charge of overseas traffic was drinking a Coca-Cola when I entered. I handed him my papers and explained my situation. He scanned them without speaking—all the time sipping the Coke. He took one long swallow, smacked his lips and belched. "Far as I can see, your travelin' papers are in order," he finally said, opening another bottle.

"Then why was I sent back here?"

"Beats me, fellow. I'm just tellin' you far as this office is concerned they're in order."

"Thank you. Now where will I contact the fighter group?" I waited. He was gurgling Coke again.

"I can only give you directions as far as Newport News, Virginia. You'll have to play it by ear from there."

"But if everything is in order why can't you be more specific?"

"I'm being as specific as I can. I'm not allowed to give out the exact location; and that's that." He belched again.

I thanked him as coldly as he had received me and left, feeling that only luck could get me to the group before it sailed.

Our plane took off in a blinding rainstorm—and it landed in another one at Norfolk, Virginia. A taxi took me to the ferry landing where I would cross over into Newport News. I sat there in the waiting room for an hour on top of my battle gear among a boisterous group of white enlisted men. Four Negro soldiers were huddled in a nearby corner. Two of them were propped against each other sleeping. Most of the white boys seemed to be making a festivity of these last hours. But there was a sort of emptiness attached to their laughing and drinking. Obviously they were headed for some departure point. It's all to hide the fear, I thought. Their faces were so young.

We filed out when the ferry whistled. It was still raining and we stood near the edge of the dock watching the boat fasten into the slip. Through the wetness I noticed a sign reading COLORED PASSENGERS and another one reading WHITES ONLY. The four black soldiers moved automatically to the colored side, and so did I. How ironic, I thought; such nonsense would not stop until we were in enemy territory.

After all the outgoing passengers were off and the trucks and cars had rumbled past, we started forward. Then I saw a Negro girl step from the ferry. She had been standing in the section marked for cars; now she was in the direct line of the white enlisted men, who stampeded to the boat screaming at the tops of their voices. I saw the girl fall beneath them into the mud and water. The four Negro soldiers also saw her go down. The five of us rushed to her rescue. She was knocked down several times before we could get to her and pull her out of the scrambling mob.

"You lousy white bastards!" one of the Negro soldiers yelled. "If I only had a gun!" Tears were in his eyes, hysteria in his voice. A long knife was glistening in his hand.

"Soldier!" I shouted above the noise, letting him get a look at my officer's cap. "Put that knife away!"

He glared at me fiercely for a second. "But you saw what they did!"

"Yes, I saw, but we're outnumbered ten to one! You can't fight all of them. Get on the boat!" He looked at me sullenly for another moment, then moved off. We cleaned the mud from the girl's coat and she walked away without a word. Only proud anger glistened on her black face. Then the four of us joined the soldier I had ordered away. He was standing still tense beneath the sign reading "colored passengers."

"Sorry, soldier," I said. "We wouldn't have had a chance against a mob like that. You realize that, don't you?"

"If I gotta die, I'd just as soon do it where I got real cause to." His tone was resolute. I had to answer. I was tempted to hand him the bit about the future and all that, but the future was too uncertain. The yelling was even louder now on the other side of the boat. "Sons-of-bitches," he muttered under his breath.

"Good luck," I said to them as we parted on the other shore. "So long," they said—except the one I had spoken to—then they moved off into the darkness and rain again. I turned away, feeling I had somehow let him down.

"Colored move to the rear!" The voice met me again when I got on the bus with some of the white enlisted men. Sick of trouble, I made my way to the back and sat down; I was the only Negro aboard. Some of the whites were standing, but I had four empty seats around me. "Gordy! My God, it's Gordy!" a voice rang out above the noise. And suddenly a soldier was rushing back toward me. "Bud!" I shouted, getting to my feet only to be knocked back to my seat by his bear hug. It was Bud Hallender, a husky man I had played basketball with back in St. Paul. Now he was down beside me, slapping my back and wringing my hands.

"You all cain't ride back there with that nigra! Move back up front where you belong!" Bud ignored the command; now he was telling the others I was the co-captain of his basketball team, his friend.

"You all hear me? You cain't ride back there with that nigra!"

"Go screw yourself!" Bud shouted back. "Drive on or we'll throw you off this goddamned crate and drive it ourselves!" Laughter rocked the bus. The driver plopped down into his seat without another word and drove off toward the heart of town. And Bud and I talked excitedly of a time and place where things had been different. Finally, at the terminal we wished each other a jovial goodbye.

I made a thorough check of my map; and, riding a hunch, I wrote out a government order for a bus ticket to a point where I suspected the pilots would be camped. The agent at the window examined it and looked at me suspiciously. "Where'd you get this?" he asked.

"It's a government issue slip, for travel."

"I know what it is, fellow, but I ain't neva heard of a nigra writin' one of these things out. I ain't givin' you no ticket. Not me."

"I'm attached to the Office of War Information. I'm my own issuing officer," I explained.

"I don't care what you are. I just don't believe no nigra can write out one of these things without a white man signing it."

"I'm en route overseas. I've got to meet my group before sailing time. I've got to catch the next bus!" My voice had risen now.

"Well, I ain't givin' you no ticket unless you got cash!" His voice was raised one notch higher than mine, and people were gathering around the window. We stood glaring at each other when a door opened on my right. "Can I be of any help to you, sir?" A young man with a pleasant face confronted me. I explained my problem and he asked me to step into his office. "Are you with an air group?" he asked after I had taken a seat.

"Yes. That's right," I answered cautiously.

"I thought so. You don't need that ticket. I have to make a telephone call. Excuse me for a moment." He came back after a few minutes. "It's all arranged. You walk straight down the main street for three blocks, turn left for two more blocks and wait there on the corner. Someone will pick you up within the next half hour."

I thanked him and went out to follow his directions, wondering whether this was a subterfuge of some kind, a way of evicting me from the terminal peacefully. I doubted it; yet such chicanery would come as no surprise now.

It was twenty minutes before an army command car rolled up beside me. A Wac stuck her head out the window and checked my description. "OWI?" she asked.

"That's right," I answered.

"Hop in," she said cheerfully. Another Wac drove the car and they whisked me off to a military barracks where my papers were thoroughly checked again, this time by an army captain.

"Have to be sure," he said, "once you're in there's no getting out." He finally handed them back with a smile. "They're okay. Good luck. Have a safe trip. The Wacs will drive you out to the embarkation base." My spirits leaped ahead of the car as we sped toward Camp Patrick Henry.

The pilots of the 332nd stopped their gambling, letter writing and drinking long enough to give me a rousing welcome. They were all genuinely happy that I had made it. My bunk had been made up and was waiting. And I showed my appreciation with two bottles of Scotch and several cartons of cigarettes which I had wrapped in my battle gear. Aside from women, I knew these were the things they would crave most. Money was useless now. They gambled it away with abandon. The noise kept up far into the night, then into morning. But I slept well, knowing the first leg of my mission had been accomplished. Now, if luck held, I would be at sea within four days.

Tony and I went out for some fresh air the next night. "It's hard to believe but we've had trouble right here on this base," he said as we walked along, "so we'd better stay in this area."

"What kind of trouble?"

"The same old jazz. One of our ground crewmen was beaten up by some white paratroopers night before last. Then they've tried to segregate us at the base's movie house. Everyone's in a hell of a mood." We became suddenly quiet as we circled the area.

A shot sounded nearby and the two of us stopped in our tracks. Then there was another shot. Someone seemed to be returning the fire. "We'd better get in. Sounds like trouble," Tony said. Our barracks had already gone dark when we entered it. Several men were at the windows with guns looking out cautiously into the night. When all was quiet again, the lights went back on and the gambling and the letter writing and the drinking started again. New orders came the following morning. We would take to the boat two days earlier than had been proposed. I was happy about this. There seemed to be less danger at sea than on this troubled base.

Colonel Davis sent for me just before noon. I hurried anxiously to his office. No more trouble, I hoped; it was too close to sailing time. But when he looked up at me his face was calm. It was, after all, some routine matter he would speak about, I thought.

"I'm sorry. Your papers are not in order. A final call from the Pentagon has come through. You will not be able to embark with us."

"This is ridiculous," I said. "Can't you do anything? Someone in Washington is trying to prevent coverage of your group overseas, Colonel. This is the first Negro fighter group. It's history. It has to be covered. Can't you protest in some way, Colonel?"

"There's nothing, absolutely nothing I can do. The orders are from the Pentagon. They cannot be rescinded. I'm terribly sorry."

I had lost. And suddenly anesthetized to the colonel and all that was around him, I turned and started out. "You are aware that you are sworn to the strictest of secrecy about what you have seen or learned here," he was saying as he followed me to the door. "You realize the dangers of any slip."

"Yes. I understand, Colonel."

"It is even possible to detain you until we are overseas under such conditions. But I am sure you won't discuss our movements with anyone."

"I won't. Don't worry. I want to forget the whole thing as quickly as possible." I rushed back toward the barracks, angry and disgusted. I couldn't bring myself to say goodbye to the pilots again. I packed quickly and waited for the command car the colonel had ordered for me.

The pilots were readying themselves for the boat when the car arrived; and I slipped through the rear door without even a backward glance. At five o'clock the next morning, after wiring Sally, I boarded a plane for Washington. I would change planes there and go on to New York, where I would wait for my wife and children. The thought of even stopping in this city irked me. I wouldn't live there again if they gave me the White House rent free, I thought as the plane roared down the runway.

We began circling over Washington at dawn; and far below I could see the landing field, lying like small strips of cardboard under a wispy patch of cloud. Further out in the distance the monuments of the city shone milk-white in the winter sunlight and the water in the mall sparkled like an oblong jewel between the sculptured trees; there was the Capitol standing quiet and strong on one end and the Lincoln Memorial set on the high quarter of the opposite slope. What a beautiful sight to be wed to such human ugliness, I thought. And as we dropped lower I could see the tops of the stores, theaters and restaurants whose doors were still closed to me.

I thought back to the fighter pilots. They would soon be far out to sea, sailing toward war and death, ignoring at least temporarily, their differences with the land they were leaving to defend. This was the price for a questionable equality.

13

FROM
Ebony Brass
by Jesse Johnson
(1914–   )

*The training of black military officers during World
War II was a delicate issue, as it had been in the past.
Although Negro leaders anticipated a battle to secure
equal and integrated training as officers, there was no pro-
longed struggle. By the middle of 1942 Negroes were
graduating from officer candidate school at the rate of approximately 200 per month, receiving commissions in
every branch of the service by the end of the war—even in
the navy and marines.*

*Jesse Johnson was born in Hattiesburg, Mississippi. He
received his B.A. from Tougaloo College in 1939 and
served with the CCC camps in Michigan for several years.
In 1942 Johnson entered the army as a private, and retired in 1962 with the rank of lieutenant colonel after
twenty years of military service. In the following selection
he describes his early life in the army and his desire to
become an officer.*

"Dress-righht-dress! Readyyyy-front! At ease."

We were in three ranks, facing one officer and several
NCO's, their feet apart, hands behind their backs, breathing regularly despite the stiff drill they had just executed.

Stretched out behind us were thousands of Negro soldiers.

"That," yelled a first sergeant, turning to us, "is the way you men will perform in six weeks. The first thing you'll have to learn is to follow orders. When you hear . . ."—I scanned the mass of marching uniforms in my line of vision upon the broad drill field while he shouted explanations at us through the fading autumn sunlight. There were several dozen officers flanking the groups. There wasn't one Negro officer. History, I thought, is repeating itself, as in all other wars—". . . less than a split second after the orders are given. If you have any big problems, this is the man to see, Captain Theodore H. Care, your company commander."

The first sergeant called the company to attention, about-faced, saluted, and was given an "at ease" by Captain Care.

A perceptible tremor passed through our lines as the words lingered in the air. Blond, blue-eyed, very white, Captain Care had a deep southern drawl.

"Before I try to make soldiers out of you," the muted words floated around us, "I want to make sure you've got one thing re-aal clear. You aren't individuals any more. You have no names and no faces. You are serial numbers, you're invisible. You're manpower . . . that's all—manpower for the U-nited States. That's the only interest I have in you."

He put his hands behind his back and strolled toward the left side of our ranks. "Most of you are northerners. You've been to school, and you think you're pretty special." He faced us again, closing one eye slightly. "Well, you're not. Got that? You're no more special than the rest of the damn . . . soldiers here."

He paused to recuperate from the near slip. Southerner or not, he couldn't afford to have three hundred men wanting him broken. But his obvious dislike for Negroes seemed to be a prime qualification for this assignment with Negro troops.

"You'll be in this company six weeks. During that time you'll be in competition with every other unit in the regiment. I expect you to win prizes. Got that? I expect you to follow orders and follow 'em damn quick. I expect you to work like a unit. You're manpower. Got that? Black manpower." He studiously avoided mention of the official view, "fighting for freedom and democracy." "We have a special place for the ones who don't follow orders!"

We got it, all right. And we understood about war. You couldn't be a somebody and a soldier at the same time. But we also understood that it wasn't war that made Captain Theodore H. Care tick; it was dislike for Negroes.

The next couple of weeks were hell. The noncoms had no easy job following Captain Care's orders. They drilled us and schooled us and tested us twelve to fourteen hours a day. Little by little, we began to look like soldiers. Basic training schedules were unusually well-organized. Every minute counted.

One evening after rifle practice, I was walking across the compound to my barrack. I heard my name called. I turned.

"Yeah, you Johnson. Don't you speak to old friends?"

I watched the figure of a man approach in the dusky light.

"Joey! For heaven's sake, what are you doing here?"

"Fighting a war, buddy. What's your excuse?"

"The same. Only mine's with the CO. Come on into the barrack while I clean my rifle."

Joey Green had worked with me in the CCC camp in Michigan. Through him I had met Captain Patterson who headed up the military side of camp with Joey as administrative assistant. When Joey's appendix ruptured, I had volunteered to give Captain Patterson a hand during my spare time from my teaching duties.

"How's the world been treating ol' Silent Sam since we parted?"

He flopped down on my bunk and pulled a cigarette from his shirt pocket.

"All right. I finished school."

"You would! How'd you finally rig it?"

"I went back to Tougaloo when I left CCC camp after a year and a half delay. They were good to me. It only took one semester."

"You know, man, I've been thinking about you lately. You're gonna make it."

"It wasn't luck. It's been a real sacrifice."

"Yeah, I guess. But you don't just sit on your backside and wait for luck. Which reminds me. I've applied for OCS."

I looked up sharply. Joey was bright. He had also done some teaching in the CCC and had two years of law school behind him. But he had never struck me as being particularly serious about anything.

"What do you think your chances are?"

He flicked an ash on the floor and shrugged. "Ixnay, I suppose. Haven't seen any Negro above a sergeant sporting a tan, even in this place. But the interview should break the monotony, anyway."

A squeal came through the loud-speakers, and Joey sat up. "Time for good little boys to hit the sack! Come over to B Company when you get a chance. We've got a girl Natzi over there . . . with rank even." He pushed against the screened door. "She's the CO's German shepherd."

A month passed before anyone had time to think about it. My turn came to send up an application for Officer

Candidate School. The envelope was bulging. Educational records, physical reports, intelligence reports, and letters of recommendation from Captain Patterson and two others.

I waited. I soldiered. I dreamed.

During the last two weeks of basic training, the psychological pressure eased off. We looked sharp, and we knew it. We had taken the prizes Captain Care wanted. We were, as he had put it, "damn good for a Negra company."

But I couldn't afford to relax. I was being watched and judged and rated every minute. All the outside rec's in the world couldn't get a man into OCS if his commanding officers didn't like him or he failed to perform up to certain accepted standards.

The constant alertness was good for me. I had reached a mental and physical peak, and I was confident.

A couple of mornings before my interview, one of my barrack mates asked me about a point of gunnery. We were in the washroom. I drew a sketch with soap on the mirror and launched into a detailed explanation. Suddenly the door swung open.

"Hey! Johnson . . . Dobber . . . come on, you guys, the whistle blew. We're forming."

The private's head disappeared. We rubbed the drying shave cream from our faces and bolted outside. D Company was in formation, tyrant Corporal Wadderman Jones in charge.

"Glad you could make it, fellas," he sneered as Dobber and I took our places. "But you needn't have rushed. We're gettin' along fine without you. In fact, just get out of line again and go over to the parade field. Several hours march under full pack might improve your hearing some."

The sun beat down on our helmets as we walked

around in a huge circle. Dust rose quickly like clouds of smoke to settle on our faces, on our brows, in our nostrils. The weight of the pack seemed to have tripled in that broiling sun. My body was drenched with sweat; but somehow my feet continued to move. About a hundred yards away, Corporal Jones shouted commands to the rest of the company.

"Pres-heent-h-arms! What's the matter with you, Hilliard? You another OCS-pusher? Shape up . . . all of you. You guys think you can goof off because you're black. Well, let me tell you, it won't work. There are a couple of bright black boys over there. Top material, one of 'em thinks. You see how far it got him. Now tighten up, Hilliard, or you'll be back plowing fields where you came from."

The boy's eyes clouded. He was young, maybe twenty. He'd been born in Alabama and his father had been lynched.

"The kid's gonna cry," Dobber whispered beside me. "I hate Jones' guts."

"Hilliard was slow," I countered in a whisper. "He deserved it."

"A lecture, maybe, but not crap stuffed down his throat." He picked up his pace and moved ahead of me.

It seemed as if I'd been walking forever and I hadn't gotten anywhere. Elizabeth was expecting me at six o'clock. The August sun bounced off the road in layers that hung around my knees.

I was going back to school in a couple of weeks, but I had to see Elizabeth first. We hadn't been together since that morning in New Orleans when she called to hear me say good-bye. I'd been job-hunting for months. It was our anniversary: two years since we'd sat on her porch after class. She was a senior at Dillard, and I'd gotten in three more semesters at Tougaloo.

My dreams of being a teacher seemed vague. The jobs I had to keep and class schedules didn't coincide. I clipped hedges, mowed the college lawns, filed test papers, and studied in the evenings.

Then one day I couldn't do it anymore. "Mental and physical fatigue," the doctor had called it. "Take a rest. Leave school."

A rest, he'd said! Going from town to town, asking every businessman in Mississippi for a job, always getting the same answer. I became a firm advocate of massive aid to education and to health.

Finally, in March 1937, I considered employment with the CCC. The Civilian Conservation Corps. . . . I had read everything available to me on this new organization. It sounded great, it was for me—for the young men of America who wanted a chance, a chance to belong, to work, to learn, to earn a monthly income. I wanted to become a part of CCC for many reasons beyond the income factor.

I stood outside the Hattiesburg, Mississippi, employment office with twenty other men, one of whom was white.

"You, in the checked shirt," called the interviewer, "come in." The white boy entered the office. Thirty minutes later he came out, smiling.

The interviewer eyed the rest of us. "What do you boys want?" Her tone was more insulting than inquisitive.

"We want to enter CCC camp, or get jobs," offered one of the men.

"Ain't takin' no applications today," she said and slammed the door. This was the state-administered federal aid picture which has existed for hundred of years.

Two days later I read a newspaper headline: "972 Mississippi Men Accepted in CCC Camps," and near the end of the article, "72 of these were Negro." I decided to go north. Mississippi gave the most assistance to those who needed it least.

It was not easy to decide to leave my home in Mississippi—the people I loved, the climate I enjoyed, the land I cherished. My total emotion was wrapped up in my surroundings. The thought of leaving aroused profound anguish. My desire to help all the people of Mississippi was serious and sincere. To be forced to leave because of race was like breaking away from one's dearest loved one, leaving a lifelong, unhealing scar within.

Elizabeth had been frightened when I boarded the train. I think she'd called up as much to talk me out of going as to say good-bye. Maybe the reports were wrong. Maybe there weren't any jobs up North either. Maybe Negroes were pushed off the sidewalks in Detroit, too.

But it was worth a try . . . anything was worth a try. And the attempt paid off. I worked with the CCC camps in Michigan nearly a year and a half before returning to Mississippi.

As I waited for a vehicle to approach, I laughed aloud. Here I was—a success, a little money in the bank,—hitching down in patched trousers to see my girl. But it didn't matter—this time I was going to finish school . . . and I wasn't going to be completely dependent on cutting hedges.

Hundreds of white people in sleek cars speeded by; a few Negroes in rattletraps putted by. It was 1938.

My thumb went out as a pickup truck rattled toward me.

"Where're you heading?" the driver asked, letting the motor idle.

"New Orleans."

"Ain't goin' that way. You live around here?"

"Yeah," I answered.

His arm shot through the window and grabbed my shirt.

"What'd you say, nigger?"

I stared blankly, feeling the collar tighten around my neck.

"I said *yes*, I live around here."

He let go of my shirt and opened the door. As he hit the ground, he pulled a truck crank from the seat.

"You said *yeah*, nigger boy. You said *yeah* to me, a white man," he yelled, striking himself on the chest and turning red.

His hand went up and I dodged. The iron bar crashed against the side of the truck. I ducked just in time to prevent murder, falling backward off balance.

There had been another man in that truck. A man who could have helped me, and didn't. A Negro man. And no help would have come from white police justice. This incident forever altered my viewpoints and plans of life. We Negroes were not protected or united in our civil rights efforts. I decided then and there to move my body north; but my soul, nearly thirty years later, is still home in Mississippi.

Even since then I have felt like an exile from his beloved land. I know the feeling of forced exile, to leave one's home, the wish to remain with friends and relatives, to be a part of the community as it grows and reaches out to offer opportunities to its youth and comfort to its aged. But a home where there is no hope, happiness, or future is a void. It is best, then, that its young sons remove themselves to find a substitute home where there is protection and opportunity.

"Jesse, the Cap'n told me to tell you you're to go before the board in fifteen minutes."

This was what I'd been waiting for: the oral review for Officer Candidate School. When I reached Headquarters there was one applicant ahead of me.

"I thought you'd already gone through this."

" 'Fraid not," answered Joey Green. "They had a lot of checking to do on me."

We sat silently for several minutes. Joey's usual exuberance was absent. He smoked steadily.

"I want this awfully much."

I listened, surprised, to the man who could laugh at being expelled from law school for having "unique and unacceptable" ideas.

"It's the only thing I ever really wanted." He looked up. "You didn't know my dad, did you? He was quite a guy . . . an Army man. He made it to sergeant in the first war. He wanted like hell to be an officer. Can you figure it? A degree in law, a member of the Pennsylvania Bar Association, and the Army board said he was too ignorant to be an officer."

Only a relatively few Negro officers were commissioned during World War I—none in the Navy. The comparative few were trained after long delays and pressures in a segregated camp in Iowa under discouraging circumstances.

He paused to light a fresh cigarette from the one already burning.

"He used to tell me that things would change by the time I grew up. I remember when he was discharged. He was lost for a long time. Nothing seemed as important as proving he could help lead the country. He said that centuries of work, blood, and tears qualified him for the all-American team. He rejected the 'Back to Africa' group, although he was proud of his African background.

"He died before I enlisted. Somebody beat him on his way home from the courthouse, working on a case in the deep South. He never regained consciousness."

The door to the conference room opened and a major called for Private Joseph E. Green.

"Good luck," I offered.

The soldier turned to me, winked, and whispered, "No, sah, Ah won't cry fo' mah mammy when the shootin' stahts."

I watched him follow the major into the room. He looked taller than usual . . . and very proud.

"Private Jesse J. Johnson."

My turn had come. Joey had been dismissed through the back door, so I didn't have a chance to find out how he thought he'd done.

Seated at an oval table were a colonel and a lieutenant colonel. The major pointed to a seat for me and joined the other officers.

"Age?"

"Twenty-seven."

"Education?"

"B.A., Tougaloo College."

"Place of birth?"

"Hattiesburg, Mississippi."

"Who was the third President of the United States?"

"Thomas Jefferson."

"What areas did U.S. troops occupy at the close of World War I?"

The questions were fired like bullets. I gave answers that would turn a history teacher gray, but I didn't flinch. They wanted reactions, not information. An officer must be alert, must reflect assurance—in convincing answers—when faced with a critical situation, as would be required in combat.

"That will be all, Private."

I saluted my six-week sharpest, about-faced, walked militarily into the afternoon sun, and returned to Army routines. On the final day of basic training, I received a letter-order from the colonel informing me of the findings of the board.

1. Pvt. Jesse J. Johnson seems qualified for Officer Candidate School and is assigned thereto.
2. Pvt. Joseph Green is not qualified for Officer Candidate School.

Before long, I thought, I'll be wearing the bars of an officer in the United States Army and shouldering responsibilities.

14

FROM
This Is My Country Too
by John A. Williams
(1925–   )

*Well-known novelist and journalist John Williams was
commissioned by* Holiday *magazine in 1963 to see if, in
fact, America was ready to accept racial tolerance. For
many months he toured the country only to find "that a
great majority of white people have no intention of sharing with black people what we have called the American
dream—unless they are forced to."*

*At one point in his trip he stopped in Grand Forks,
North Dakota, to talk to some people at the Strategic Air
Command Base. He interviewed a number of Negro airmen who poured out their frustration and anguish in the
hope that Williams could do something to make their
lives more bearable—despite a white lieutenant's assurance that "we don't have any racial problems here."*

There is not much to do in the cities and towns of the
northern plains. Night comes with a thudding finality,
and the restaurants and bars are usually quiet places
where a man can reflect on his day, or escape reflection
on anything. The Russians are the big bad boys out there.
One headline spoke of Mr. Khrushchev with the in-
formality of the New York *Daily News: NIKITA*

WARNS OF MORE CONVOY CRISES. After the success of TV team reporting, a la Huntley-Brinkley, I suppose it was natural that this style would become the vogue, especially with NBC-TV affiliates. But, to use the tandem announcers to report city budgets and traffic accidents and anticipated thousands doing Christmas shopping seemed to me ludicrous and pretentious. However, there it was. You could tell the stations that had money, for they ran film on their news shows; the poorer ones used stills and narration.

I had passed places where snow had fallen, but none came down while I trekked the northern plains. There was rain. For days the sky was overcast. Sometimes rain came down, sometimes it didn't, but always threatened to. Mornings were never pleasant now and the driving itself became monotonous, with flat, black earth spread all around and only a dun-colored hillock to break the monotony from time to time. My beautiful new car was spattered with mud and dirt; its value was now purely utilitarian, for there was no sun to show off its beauty. Except for the cars on the road and the occasional town and one passenger train I saw rounding a great curve outside Duluth, the earth seemed uninhabited. I took a side road and it got worse. By the time I arrived on the outskirts of Grand Forks, North Dakota, I was mentally beat and needed something to life my spirits.

It was in 1960 that I had heard some ugly stories about Grand Forks, the kind of stories that were so commonplace in America during World War II that after a while they stopped being news at all. I wanted to see the town and talk to some Air Force people at the nearby Strategic Air Command base. The town itself was small, misshapen, and gray; it sat upon the plain apologetically. Most of the buildings and homes appeared to be made of wood. I checked into one of those motels that still pay tribute to the old West. There was a corral, hitching posts, and of course the bunkhouse. I lunched quickly, got directions to the air base, and got behind the horses once more.

At the gate of the SAC base, the guard looked at my authorization very carefully. He was from Virginia, his duty plate showed, and had a heavy accent. When he called the Public Information Officer, I believe he wanted to say, "There's a colored fella out here." But he looked at me once—I was standing close to the phone—and made the call straight.

When I walked into the PIO office, a sergeant asked me to wait because the lieutenant was out. A Negro airman, second class, sat at a desk across the room, trying to stifle a smile. He winked a couple of times. I made a note to talk to him. I had heard that prejudice and discrimination in Grand Forks were not at all unlike some Southern cities. I wanted to know what it was like for a Negro airman to live there. I wanted to know, for my sons lean toward the Air Force and because I am concerned about this world being blown up by some madman. I am concerned whether that nut is black or white. I wouldn't be at all happy to know that a Negro, enraged by prejudice, crazed by discrimination, decided to take his hurts out on everyone, but we are well within the realm of that possibility.

Suddenly everyone in the office found things to do after the sergeant gave me a copy of the base paper, the *Peace Garden Trident*.

"Where you from?" the Negro asked me.

"New York."

"Manhattan?"

"Yes."

"I'm from Brooklyn." He smiled and winked once more. Surely he had something to tell me.

"Where you staying?"

"Motel about eighteen miles back toward town."

"I know that one. How long you going to be around?"

"Until tomorrow."

"Like wrinkled steaks?"

"Wrinkled what?"

"Chitlins."

"Chitlins? In North Dakota? Yes."

"My wife and I are having them for dinner. Come on over."

There was the nice thing I wanted to happen.

When the Information Officer, a tall young man with a slightly pitted face and undistinguished brown hair, came in, he was dogged by a reporter from the Minneapolis *Tribune*. There had been a brawl in town involving some airmen. One of the airmen was critically injured and in the hospital. Were the airmen Negro? After some anxious moments, I learned they were not. I was relieved. While the lieutenant and I talked, I was conscious of the Negro airman smiling his secret smile. Did no one else see it? When the officer's room was clear of the reporter, we went in. At first I tried to discuss the routine things such as "offensive posture," how long it took to get the bombers off (15 minutes), the establishment of Minuteman Intercontinental Ballistic Missile sites on the base, the Hound Dog, which the bombers carried.

"Since the emphasis on being ready to go in is just as important as living normally, there must be some mental conflict among the crewmen. How many—"

"The crews are watched every minute on their four-day alert," the lieutenant assured me.

"How many psychiatric cases do you have in, say, a year?"

"Don't know offhand, but those people don't get up.

Every man in the crew watches the other men. Each one is carefully and routinely checked out."

"You had a severe housing and racial problem here a couple of years ago. How's it go now?"

Without pausing he said, "We have three hundred new base houses. They take care of seventeen hundred family units. We don't have any racial problems here. The town's wide open. Our boys get along all right."

We'll see, I thought while he was issuing a pass and assigning the young Negro airman to take me around. We went downstairs and got into my car. He drove. As we went down the road he turned to me and smiled. "You shook 'em up in there."

"How do you mean?"

"The sergeant didn't know what to do with you. That's why he gave you a copy of the paper. I'm one of the editors. And the lieutenant didn't know what to make of it all. When the call came in that there was a guy out there from *Holiday,* we expected—you know, a white guy. Then you came in—" He started to laugh.

The airman was in his early twenties, a nice-looking kid. He went on, "I don't know why the lieutenant sent you out with me. He wasn't using his head, you shook him up so much. There's a lot going on here."

"Like what?"

"It's a bitch here!" We passed through gate after gate, pausing to show the pass to the guards. "I'll let you talk to some of the guys. Don't use my name though, I'm getting out in January. After that, I just don't give a damn, but they might take it out on my friends who still have time to pull."

We cruised down the flight line and I stared at the silver birds squatting there. I interrupted the airman's bored monologue describing the planes, their capabilities, to ask, "Where's the lieutenant from with that accent?"

"Michigan, but the whole damned place is filled with accents, mostly from the South. Crackers all over the joint."

We arrived at the Guidance Control Center, a cement and steel building, rather like a vault, a mortuary, with most of the space given over to banks of computers, long, dark, formidable-looking objects. A staff sergeant explained the functions of the computers, but I could not fully absorb all the things these machines could do. Nor could I really comprehend why the planes were out on the line, heavy winged with fuel, the Hound Dogs nestled in their armpits. The readiness of it all stunned me. SAC says in some of its material: "If a SAC bomber or missile is ever launched in anger towards an enemy . . . SAC will have failed to carry out its objective of preserving the peace." To be ready for war is to be ready for war, and the fine slogans do not obscure that fact. But strangely, I had the feeling, seeing airmen striding up and down the walks, that they believed the slogans.

When the sergeant in computing turned me loose, my head swimming, the airman from the PIO office led me outside. It had been gray all day with spotty rain in the morning; it had stopped about noon. Now, it was coming down again as we stood, getting wet. With my guide was another Negro. He didn't wait for introductions. He said, "Can you help us?"

The Control Center framed his leaning, slender figure. Behind me was the flight line and I thought to myself, No, not twenty years later, *still*. But I fenced, I fished for my illusion. "What is it?"

He saw through that stupid question and did not embarrass me. Because it was raining, I thought suddenly of Greg and Dennis; it had been raining when I said good-bye to them. Can I help? What could I say? What could I do, no matter how exciting the prospects of tackling the entire Force? The second airman flushed livid. He was dark, and now his skin took on an ugly, purple color. He began ticking off on his fingers: "We get the lousiest houses in town. We can only be served in two or three restaurants. Our officers, mostly from the South, don't back us up; they don't even care."

"What about the Negro officers?" I asked. The sergeant who had shown me the computing systems passed and the airmen waited until he was out of earshot.

"Nearly all of them are on the crews, and they stick to themselves as if it couldn't touch them. Once in a while some cracker get drunk and calls them 'niggers' in the officers' club; everybody laughs for a week."

My guide spoke now: "We get the stiffest sentences, bar none, for minor infractions. And don't let something happen with the cops in town. They'd forget all about us out here. The white guys really get upset when we have dances and some of the colored guys bring white girls from Winnipeg. We've had one or two rumbles already. They hush those up right quick. There are no colored women here, except the wives and daughters of the personnel. The single guys go all the way to Winnipeg when they have time off rather than hang around this dog-ass, Jim Crow town."

"Your congressman?" I asked.

The second airman was also from New York and lived in Adam Clayton Powell's district. He turned his face up to the wetting skies in disgust and shifted his feet. "We wrote to Powell and he checked around; some brass told him it wasn't so, and that was that." He spread his legs and placed his hand on his hips. "Look, you can use my name, that's how much I don't give a damn anymore."

I felt fatherly when I said, "No, you don't want to do that." But I knew the feeling. God, how I knew the feeling, the feeling so many young Negroes now have. Let the body become the object of opposition; let them move it; let them take your life, if they will, but get there, all of you, mind and body.

For me it boiled down to a conference with a personnel officer one day, on Guam, and he suggested that, as requested by the commander of the new outfit I was in (an outfit disgustingly fresh from the States), I move into the quarters of the steward mates, who were all Negro. I was a pharmacist's mate and until then had shared a tent with two other pharmacist's mates who had been transferred into the outfit with me. I refused to move, was given a speedy court-martial for disobeying orders, and summarily sentenced to five days' bread and water in a Marine brig. But there were formalities. I had to be checked to see if my health was good. I was running a temperature, malaria, and they dumped me in the sick bay. However, to circumvent my suspended sentence, they came to take my temperature in the morning, when fevers usually run low. They found my temperature near normal and hauled me off to the brig, where dry shaves were the order of the day. We had to walk three miles for our bread and water, even the guys who were chained together. We had one cigarette after each "meal," had it standing in line. Some of us became dizzy from them, spaced as they were. Japanese prisoners of war gave us cigarettes and candy. Naturally, most of the American prisoners were Negro.

So I knew the feeling.

"I don't give a damn," the second airman repeated. I was plunging through panic. By the time I wrote of my trip to Grand Forks, this kid might have already blown his top.

My guide said, "You get a traffic violation in town and your picture gets in the paper, but not a white airman."

"Please, can't you do something?" the second airman said, with the air of one who is prepared to take matters into his own hands.

"I'll do what I can," I said, shaking his hand and feeling as useless as hell. Jesus Christ, what do I tell my sons now?

Kennedy would do something, my guide said, when we got back into the car. "When he was out here, he reached over people to shake my hand." He looked at me as though daring me to dispute his statement.

"I'm sure he would do something," I said.

He was through for the day and we drove to my motel and opened a bottle. I placed a call to Bob Johnson at *Jet*, told him what I had learned, and he promised to get a man up there as soon as possible. "Not right away," he said, "can't, but tell them cats up there to hang on in there, hear?"

It was night now and it closed fiercely over the town. We drove along the straight stretch of road into town, to my guide's home. He lived in a ramshackle building; the rooms he and his wife shared were matchboxes; the ceilings and walls were done in cheap paint over buckling walls. The place came furnished, but the furniture must have been carted from England at the height of the Victorian period; there was hardly room to pass between the chair and couch in the living room.

"What do you pay?"

"Eighty-five a month, on my salary. And we looked for seven months."

The chitlins were good, but we ate off a card table.

"So we can fold it up and make believe that there's more room than we actually have," the young wife said. She was a nurse in town, and hated it. "I've been here for months, but they still treat me like I'm some kind of freak."

Just as we finished, four Negro airmen in civilian clothes came in.

"Where you guys going?" my guide asked.

"To a movie," one of them said. "Do you know, we've never been to a movie in this town. We don't even know if they'll let us in or not, but we're going to try. Safety in numbers, you know." They all grinned. As they filed out the door, one turned and said, "Sure hope you can do something, Mr. Williams."

"Man, he's already started," my guide said with a laugh. "He called *Jet* two hours ago."

"Yeah?"

"Yeah!"

So much faith in *Jet?* I don't know. When they went out, they went out smiling; they hadn't come in that way. A man in Athens once asked me why black Americans had their own magazines. Weren't they Americans too? And I had to reply that too often the black American does not see his image in the American press—thus, Negro publications.

The airman agreed to take me around the town, and we drove through streets filled with Christmas shoppers. In a club we found another group of Negro airmen. This was one of the clubs that would serve them. "Is this another safety group?" I asked.

"Goddamn right," one of them said. The club was a dark and dingy place, and as we were about to leave, some musicians climbed on the stand and started placing chairs. One looked like a Negro.

"That guy," my guide said, "has been passing for an Indian for years, they tell me. He gets along with everybody. Doesn't he look like a brother to you?"

He did indeed.

Later my guide took me around the town, pointing out places whose windows ordinarily carried signs that read: *Indians and Colored not allowed.* But it was dark; the signs were small, and I didn't see them. Only the places where I was told they were. As we walked, we came upon a pinch-faced woman pushing a baby in a stroller. She slowed, as if demanding that we move off the sidewalk. When we didn't she drew up her skinny frame and came straight ahead, looking neither right nor left. The stroller struck my ankle as she passed. I thought, You little bitch!

We passed beneath the Christmas lights strung along two or three short blocks in the center of Grand Forks. Merry Christmas.

15

"Armed Defense"
An Interview with Charles R. Sims

*Once again American Negroes feel the need to band to-
gether for self defense against their own countrymen.
The Deacons, formed for this purpose, are rightly called
black soldiers. They subscribe to the same constitutional
prerogatives as the Black Panthers, and are subjected to
the same intimidations and harassments.*

*When this interview took place in 1965, Charles Sims
was the president of the Bogalusa, Louisiana, chapter of
Deacons for Defense and Justice. He was interviewed by
William Price, a reporter for the* National Guardian,
where this following selection originally appeared.

Q. Mr. Sims, why do you feel there is need for the
Deacons in the civil rights movement and in Bogalusa?

A. First of all, the reason why we had to organize the
Deacons in the city of Bogalusa was the Negro people
and civil rights workers didn't have no adequate police
protection.

Q. Can you tell us what difference it may have made
in Bogalusa to have the Deacons here?

A. Well, when the white power structure found out
that they had mens, Negro mens that had made up their
minds to stand up for their people and to give no ground,
would not tolerate with no more police brutality, it had

a tendency to keep the night-riders out of the neighborhood.

Q. You say the Deacons were formed because you were not given adequate police protection, does this mean that you consider the role of the Deacons to be a sort of separate police organ in behalf of the civil rights movement?

A. Well, I wouldn't say policemen, I would say a defense guard unit. We're not authorized to carry weapons.

Q. You say you're not authorized to carry weapons?

A. No we're not.

Q. Can you tell me how the Deacons view the use of weapons?

A. Self-protection.

Q. Do most Deacons, in their efforts to protect the civil rights movement, would they normally carry a gun or a pistol with them?

A. That's the only way you can protect anything, by having weapons for defense. If you carry weapons, you carry them at your own risk.

Q. Do the local authorities object to your carrying weapons?

A. Oh yeah, the local, the federal, the state, everybody object to us carrying weapons, they don't want us armed, but we had to arm ourselves because we got tired of the women, the children being harassed by the white night-riders.

Q. Have they done anything to try to get the weapons away from you?

A. Well, they threatened several times. The governor even said he was going to have all the weapons confiscated, all that the state troopers could find. But on the other hand, the governor forgot one thing—in an organization as large as the Deacons, we also have lawyers and we know about what the government can do. That would be unconstitutional for him just to walk up and start searching cars and taking people's stuff without cause.

Q. Has there been a court case to determine this?

A. No.

Q. The Second Amendment to the United States Constitution guarantees the right of the people to carry weapons, is that the way you feel about it, that the people have a right to carry weapons in their own self-defense?

A. I think a person should have the right to carry a weapon in self-defense, and I think the Louisiana state law says a man can carry a weapon in his car as long as it is not concealed. We found out in Bogalusa that that law meant for the white man, it didn't mean for the colored. Any time a colored man was caught with a weapon in his car, they jailed him for carrying a concealed weapon. So we carried them to court.

Q. It's your understanding then, that a person possessing a gun in his home, or carrying it in his car, that this is within your rights?

A. According to law it is.

Q. When you confront a white man with a weapon as compared with confronting a white man without a weapon, could you tell us what the difference in the white man's reaction is; as to whether or not you are armed, or unarmed?

A. Well, I want to say when *I* confront a white man, I would be just as dangerous to the white man without a weapon as I would be with a weapon, if he didn't treat me right.

Q. But suppose he had a weapon, and you didn't?

A. Then he'd have the better hand.

Q. When the Deacons carry weapons, do they do this with any thought to use these in any way except in self-defense?

A. No man a member of the Deacons will attack any-one, he has to use his weapons in defense only.

Q. Have there been any examples of the actual use of weapons by the Deacons, have you ever had to use them?

A. I would rather not answer that.

Q. Can you tell me what difference it has made with the white community, the fact that there are the Deacons here in Bogalusa and that they are prepared to use arms even if they may not?

A. For one thing that made a difference, there were a lot of night-riders riding through the neighborhood; we stopped them. We put them out and gave them fair warning. A couple of incidents happened when people were fired on. So the white man right away found out that a brand new Negro was born. We definitely couldn't swim and we was as close to the river as we could get so there was but one way to go.

Q. So you think there has been a difference in the attitude of the white people toward the civil rights movement in Bogalusa because you have been here to protect it?

A. Yes, I do believe that. I believe that if the Deacons had been organized in 1964, the three civil rights workers that was murdered in Philadelphia, Mississippi, might have been living today because we'd have been around to stop it.

Q. Do the Deacons have any code or any instructions or any policy about the use of arms, about when they will use them?

A. Yes, we have our by-laws that each man must study to make sure that he understands them and must abide by them before he can become a Deacon.

Q. Is there anything you can say about the pledge that a Deacon takes, or the oath?

A. He pledges his life for the defense of justice, that's

one thing he do, for the defense of the Negro people, and the civil rights workers in this area. When I say this area, that doesn't necessarily mean Bogalusa, that's anywhere we're needed in this vicinity.

Q. You mean in this parish?

A. That's right, and if necessary, out of this parish.

Q. What has been the response to the existence of the Deacons from the civil rights movement, from the Congress of Racial Equality, other civil rights organizations or from unaffiliated whites that come in like we might come in?

A. They're most glad we have the Deacons organized. See, right now it's rather quiet. Two months ago a white civil rights worker or even a colored civil rights worker, he couldn't come into Bogalusa unless we brought him in. The whites would be on the road trying to stop cars. We've taken on the job of transportation in and out of Bogalusa, bringing people backwards and forwards, making sure that they get here safe.

Q. Is this to protect against truckloads of whites, night-riders and that sort of thing?

A. Anybody that tries to get next to the civil right workers, anybody.

Q. Can you tell me what kind of weapons are preferred, is it a shotgun or a rifle or a pistol?

A. A shotgun is for close range stuff. I don't intend to let a man get close enough to me to hit me with a shotgun.

Q. So you prefer a rifle?

A. The best that they make.

Q. Do you have any recommendations for white people travelling in the South?

A. Yes, be careful. And if you're a civil rights worker, don't let nobody know it.

Q. Would you recommend that white persons interested in or working in the civil rights movement carry their own arms or guns when they travel in the South?

A. I will not recommend anyone to carry guns. I don't think that's my job to recommend people to carry weapons. When you carry a weapon, you have to have a made-up mind to use it. I am president of the Deacons and not a legal advisor to everyone who passes through Bogalusa.

Q. Can you tell us anything about how you would operate in any kind of an emergency situation? Would you get a call by phone, or do you have a two-way radio set up? Suppose something was happening to somebody in an outlying district, how are you likely to know about it and how are you likely to respond to it?

A. The old saying that I've heard is that bad news travels fast. We have telephones, naturally, word of mouth, and we have some powerful walkie-talkies. We can receive a lot of different calls on the walkie-talkies that we can't transmit, but we can receive them. And that's what bugs the white man today, why was we able to be in so many places so quick. We was intercepting their calls.

Q. You were intercepting the calls of the white people?

A. Sure, the Ku Klux Klan, sometimes the police calls, all depends.

Q. You mean they have their own radios and you listen in to them?

A. Naturally.

Q. Could you give any kind of example of a situation like this?

A. There are so many of them, I don't know which one to pick out.

Q. Could you pick one where you got, say, a call from out of town and you had to go out there real quick?

A. Yes, we had a doctor coming into Bogalusa and they dropped him off in Covington. We received a call that peoples down there were asking him a lot of questions and we had to get to Covington quick, and get him out of there. That's about 28 miles. So about 16–17 minutes after I received a call, I pulled up at the gas station. When I pulled up at the gas station—well, I knew the doctor—and I had two carload of mens, maybe ten mens. And I walked up and picked up his bag and said, "Let's go Doc," well two, three white boys started behind him. And I just turned around and said, "Partner, if you want to keep living you better go back, because if you come any closer to this car, I'm going to kill all three of you." I wasn't going to kill them; it was just a threat. So we had to bring Doc out and had to hurry up and get him out. So down the road we had two–three peoples tried to follow us, but we have some pretty fast automobiles. They're a little faster than the usual car.

Q. When you confronted the white people there at the service station, did you show a weapon at that point?

A. I didn't have to—they know me. I showed my face. That was weapons enough. And they know wherever they see me, my gun and the Deacons are close.

Q. The mere showing of a weapon, does that sometimes take care of a situation?

A. The showing of a weapon stops many things. Everybody want to live and nobody want to die. But here in Bogalusa, I'm one of the few peoples who is really known as a Deacon and anybody that I associate with, they just take for granted they are Deacons. I show up; then ten, twelve more mens show up, whether they Deacons or not, they branded, you know. That make the white man respect us even more, because nine out of ten he be right.

Q. There might be some people who feel that merely by your having weapons in your possession and being willing to use them, that this might create violence rather than stopping it. . . .

A. Well some peoples ought to take one other thing into consideration. I owned three or four weapons long before the civil rights movement. I went to jail, I think about three times for carrying concealed weapons ten years before the movement start. So, I mean, having a weapon's nothing new. What bugged the people was something else—when they found out what was the program of the Deacons. I do have a police record.

Q. Do you want to talk about it?

A. It's no secret. Every time I went to jail it was for carrying a weapon or battery. I've never been to jail for drunks, stealing or nothing like that. But I used to fight all the time and when they discovered I was president of the Deacons, they looked up my record and checked how many times I whipped white boys on the biggest street they have in the city and I wasn't afraid of the law or nobody else they start thinking twice. It's good that they did because I meant business. I had made up my mind.

Q. If you say that the white man was not bugged until the Deacons were created, was it the organization of a group like the Deacons that made the difference rather than, say, you as an individual. . . .

A. No, not me as an individual. See, the Southern white man is almost like Hitler in the South. He been dictating to the Negro people, "Boy, this," and "Uncle, that," and "Granma, go here," and people's been jumpin'. So he gets up one morning and discovers that "Boy," was a man, and that he can walk up and say something to "Boy" and "Boy" don't like what he say, he tell him to eat himself—you know? And then if he blow up, there's a good fight right there. So the man goes back home and sit down and try to figure out the Negro. Shortly after that we had several rallies. And I guess he received his answer—we told him a brand new Negro was born. The one he's been pushin' around, he didn't exist anymore.

Q. Do you think people here in Bogalusa realize that now?

A. Oh, yes.

Q. Has it made a difference?

A. A great difference.

Q. Could you describe the difference?

A. First of all we don't have these people driving through this neighborhood throwing at people's houses, catching two or three fellows on the streets, jumping out their car, whipping them up 'cause these are Negroes and they are white. We don't be bothered because these paddies [whites] in the streets calling themselves collectors harassing the womens and going from door to door to see 'how that one is.' We don't have any of this. Because of the Deacons, we don't have any of this. We don't have much work to do now. But up until the middle of July we patrolled the streets 24 hours a day, and made sure we didn't have any of this. When we found this, we hadded 'em up and if they give us any resistance, we, you know, shook 'em up.

Q. What do you mean, "Shook 'em up?"

A. Well you know how to shake a man up, you know. Teach him that you mean business.

Q. Where we come from, that might be called "roughing him up."

A. Well, yes, a little Bogart, you know. Pop him up

the side of his head, shake him up, take his weapon away from him and show him the way to get back to town.

Q. Has anyone ever been arrested for doing that?

A. No. One boy was arrested, he was accused of drawing a gun on a man, accused of it. It was two weapons against him and eight weapons for him. Now if a judge is trying you for something you done to me, even though you's guilty, if you have two mens in your defense and eight against you, who should the judge respect?

Q. I think *you* better answer that question.

A. The majority witnesses. And if he don't, we move it to a higher court until we find a court that respect the fact that eight people's word should be greater than two.

Q. Except for yourself, the names of the other Deacons are not known. . . .

A. Only about four.

Q. Now outside of Bogalusa, when there is some news about a Negro carrying a gun or about some kind of violence, and people don't know who the Deacons are and who may not be Deacons, they may feel that this is the Deacons at work. Have there been instances like that where there has been violence and the Deacons were blamed for it?

A. Yes, a lot of cases. Any time a Negro and a white man have any kind of a round up and the Negro decide he going to fight him back, he's a Deacon. We had one case here where a Negro and a white man had a round and a little shootin' was done. He was named a Deacon. Now I can truthfully say he was not a Deacon. But the papers, the government and everybody else say he was. So I laugh at the government to its face. I told them point blank, you do not know who Deacons is and quit gettin' on the air and telling peoples that people are Deacons just because they stood up to a white man.

Q. If no one knows who the Deacons are except you. . . .

A. I didn't say except me, the secretary have to know— he keep the records.

Q. So the known Deacons are yourself and the secretary?

A. No, myself, the vice-president who is Roy N. Burris, weighs 116 pounds soaking wet but he's a man. Another man's name I will not give you because he's leaving. And Robert Hicks, he's public relations man for the Deacons.

Q. If the membership is not known, would you call it a secret society?

A. As far as the white man is concerned, yes.

Q. Could you say how many Deacons there are in Bogalusa and throughout the South?

A. No, but I'll tell you this, we have throughout the South at this time somewhere between 50 and 60 chapters.

Q. Roughly how many people in each chapter.

A. I won't tell you that.

Q. Could you tell us what areas they cover?

A. Alabama, Mississippi, Arkansas, Louisiana, Texas.

Q. Georgia?

A. No. We have Georgia and North Carolina in mind. As a matter of fact I was supposed to go to North Carolina and organize the people there, and in Florida, but I don't have time right now to do it.

Q. Have you been making trips outside of Louisiana to see these other groups, to help them organize?

A. No, I send mens. And the headquarters in Jonesboro sends mens out.

Q. The headquarters is in Jonesboro, Louisiana.

A. Yes.

Q. Is Jonesboro near Bogalusa?

A. No, it's about 300 miles from here, way up North in Louisiana.

Q. Near the Arkansas border?

A. Shouldn't be too far.

Q. Could you tell us what views you might have on the civil rights tactics of non-violence?

A. The non-violent act is a good act—providing the policemens do their job. But in the Southern states, not just Louisiana, but in the Southern states, the police have never done their job when the white and the Negro are involved—unless the Negro's getting the best of the white man.

Q. How do you think the movement could best be advanced or get its aims the quickest if it didn't use non-violence?

A. I believe non-violence is the only way. Negotiations are going to be the main point in this fight.

Q. Would it be correct to put it this way, that you feel non-violence is the correct way to get political and economic things done. . . .

A. Sure.

Q. But that behind that, behind the non-violence, the Deacons or organizations like the Deacons are necessary to protect the rights of this non-violent movement?

A. That's right.

Q. Do you find a noticeable change, not necessarily in the police here, but generally in the white people in this town that comes because they know there are people ready to defend the civil rights movement? Are they taking on some second thoughts?

A. Sure—who wouldn't? If you'd been walking down the streets doing anything you want and all at once you find out that you can't go down that street like you used to, wouldn't you make a change?

Q. Mr. Sims, just one last question, how long do you think the Deacons will be needed in the civil rights movement?

A. First of all, this is a long fight. In 1965 there will be a great change made. But after this change is made, the biggest fight is to keep it. My son, his son might have to fight this fight and that's one reason why we won't be able to disband the Deacons for a long time. How long, Heaven only knows. But it will be a long time.

16

FROM
G.I. Diary
by David Parks
(1944–   )

David Parks, son of photographer Gordon Parks, whose experiences twenty-five years and two wars earlier have already been described, saw service in Vietnam. His diary, portions of which are reprinted here, is convincing evidence that while the enemy may have changed and methods of warfare may be more modern, discrimination and racial bigotry are just the same as they were a quarter century ago.

Parks confides that after induction "most of the Negro fellows . . . worry most about being sent down South. I worry, too. I'd rather freeze the rest of the winter than do my basic in Dixie." What kind of country is this where a white American is a greater threat to a Negro American soldier than a North Vietnamese? Parks wonders about the justice of it all. "Read about the riots in the States . . . they leave me confused . . . it makes me wonder whether we're fighting the right war."

December 8, 1965
Drill—drill—drill. March—march—march. I've had it. Got to be a good soldier if I want to get home for Christ-

mas. Drew KP duty for tomorrow. More pots and pans. [Sgt.] Crouch is beginning to make it tough for several of us souls.

Very few Negroes here and only a few of them non-coms. I'm wondering how some of the Southern white boys will take orders from them. There are lots of them from Georgia, Alabama and Mississippi. They never speak to me. I tried breaking the ice with one the other day. I asked him how he liked the army. He just gave me an evil look and turned away. It got to be a game with me. I asked another one the same question on the PT course this morning. "That's my business," he said. I've decided they're not worth being curious about.

We've got nice new barracks here, built about two years ago. Each floor has two large rooms divided into cubicles that accommodate two people. I'm on the third floor with a good view of the Kansas plains out my window. My roommate is a white kid from Missouri. Nice but strange. No liquor, no smoking, no women. He's very shy and soft-spoken and reads the Bible every night. Somehow I feel he's not cut out for army life, but who is? He's absent-minded, so he catches hell all the time. I feel sorry for him. But who knows, he's liable to make a damn good soldier when combat time comes around.

December 18, 1965

Life here is so dull there's nothing to write about. Am going home on a fourteen-day leave next week. Great!

January 7, 1966

Yesterday's march wasn't that bad. It turned out to be a ten-mile, forced night march. My feet hurt. There was a sudden mock attack by men from the other platoons, who were considered to be the "enemy" catching us by surprise. They hid in bushes and waited until we marched past them. Then they began firing blanks and phony explosive charges. It was a little hairy at first, but it turned into fun after a while. One GI was shot with a blank and received a small burn. Nothing serious. It did make you think of what Vietnam will be like. I fired very well on the range earlier in the day. I might turn out to be a sharpshooter.

January 8, 1966
 The fellows in my platoon are becoming nicer guys. It's about time, over five weeks now. Maybe it's because they are making a team of us, getting us to realize we will have to depend upon one another in combat. A white guy from New York, who hadn't known Negroes before, said he feels we are no different from his own people. He feels that a lot of the other white guys are beginning to feel the same way. Big deal.

 The commanding officer thinks our platoon is the best in the company. He said last night that if he had our company for six months more, he would take us into battle. I guess we really proved ourselves on that march. Crouch thinks differently. He always does when it comes to us. He's a real prickhead. He's from New York and thinks he knows how most of us from there shape up. Some fellows say he was a failure on the outside. He's a pain in the ass, a mean bastard, and getting meaner every day.

 My roommate seemed better today. Got two letters from home. He read each one of them several times, then stuck them in his Bible. He's as quiet as a tombstone. I don't know why, but I feel sorry for him.

 Training is moving fast now. Lots of studying and class after class. They work us harder than the average college student. But there's a reason. We are learning how to kill, while the college student is learning how to live. Damn, this place is getting me down. Suddenly everything seems so distorted. Home doesn't seem real any more.

January 11, 1966

The sergeant asked a tough question today. He wanted to know if we were ready to kill. I've thought about this for a long time now. I don't know. I don't think so. But I got my sharpshooter rating today, 38 out of 45 targets. It felt good. A lot of the guys didn't even come close.

This getting up at four in the cold is a drag. If you can conquer this weather, you can make it anywhere. It's damn cold and lonesome at that time of the morning. We pile into the trucks and ride like sardines in a can. Range firing goes on until about six. Sometimes we walk back about twelve miles to camp. This morning we were so tired most of us crawled into the barracks. Literally.

Got a letter from Marie Ann today. She has a beautiful heart and mind. I can't wait to see her again.

January 26, 1966

Crouch got me. It's KP for me this weekend.

Nine days until leave, and things are moving fast. We crawled the combat assault course today, moving down lanes and firing at stationary targets. This was a team effort. While one line fired, the other line advanced. It got a bit hairy at times because some guys fired out of their lanes.

January 27, 1966

Combat firing again early this morning. Damn, it was cold, at least ten degrees below zero. They must be training us to fight Eskimos. My fingers were so cold I thought they had fallen off. At one point I had a crazy feeling that they were on fire. Got scared as hell once when I couldn't button my fly. If things around there had got frostbite,

I'd have been in real trouble. My feet haven't thawed out yet. Ten hours of this kind of crappy weather makes a man think about going AWOL. Some of the guys were actually crying. They had turned blue. One very dark soul brother complained that he was turning white. A cracker from the South laughed and said, "Boy, it ain't ever gonna get that cold." I wanted to put my boot up his behind, but down inside me I had to laugh. As we walked back to the trucks, one group would chant, "Sound off! Sound off!" The others would answer, "Pissed off! Pissed off!"

January 29, 1966

It's still below zero out there. They're drilling for those boring parades. Screw it. I'm on sick call. I got my behind caught up in some barbed wire last night on the tactics course. Shea had to free me. He was laughing so hard it took him over five minutes. Crouch told me if I let that happen in Vietnam, Charlie would have my ass for chow.

Three AWOLs are still missing. They can't find them. FBI probably after them by now. A few of our guys were thinking about going over the hill, but we talked them out of it. Only one week to go and a lot of guys still aren't adjusted. It's too late now for that kind of jazz. Uncle Samuel's got us for the next twenty-two months.

February 26, 1966

They changed my MOS (Military Occupation Specialty) today. They've put me in a nuclear jeep group temporarily. Don't know much about it right now. Sgt. Groper is over here with us, so we'll have some sexy marching cadences. We won't start individual training for another week. So there will be nothing but work details until then.

March 4, 1966

Well, the shit has started again. I'm totally pissed off today. First of all it's my birthday, and for a present I drew KP. This is my third time this week, and you're only supposed to pull it once every two weeks. Another Negro guy got the same treatment. His name is Allgood. Says the sergeant has been giving it to him and another soul ever since they've been at Funston. This white sergeant, Morris, is the one who is pouring it on. Doesn't like the way I dress, stand, walk or talk. He stays on my back. Like in formation this morning he singles me out; "Parks, you look like you just came off a block in Harlem."

"Why, Sergeant?" I asked. "What gives you that impression?"

"I know your kind, man. You're all the same," he says.

"You mean all the recruits?"

He looks at me hard. "Naw. I mean you-all. And you oughta know what you-all means. Not git down and give me ten push-ups." I still don't know what he meant, but I gave him the ten push-ups. On the tenth one I gave him a jolt. I let out a fart that you could hear all the way to the Oklahoma border. The whole line broke up with laughter. Well, that's how I pulled KP. This place is becoming a bigger bore every day. What a hell of a way to come into your twenty-second year.

March 7, 1966

I don't know where most of these guys in my barracks were trained. They have the worst habits I've ever seen. They pick their noses and wear the same socks and underwear all week. The place really smells terrible. Three-fourths of them are from the South and have lousy diction. I thought Allgood, the soul from Mississippi, spoke bad enough, but these crackers make him sound like an English major from Oxford. They're clannish, too. Seldom ever speak to me. I lucked up on a good roommate. A white guy named Posthorn from Sheboygan, Wisconsin. He's nice, talks slow and quiet like, walks slow and never bothers anybody. He just takes it easy and goes along with the program—which I would like to do if these bastards would stop making my program so tough.

March 10, 1966

Strange, I'm beginning to have more self-confidence. Maybe it's because I resent the army thinking for me. I don't like being pushed around. Never had such bad feelings against white guys before either. But then I've never met white guys like these before. They don't let you forget that you're colored and that they're white for one minute. I've never thought so much about color before, even at school when I was the only soul. The question of color never comes up at home. Everyone is treated the same. I'd like to take one of these cats home with me and let him get an eyeful. Ever since I was a kid our backyard has looked like the United Nations. Well, I'll see what these fair-skinned brothers do when we're under fire. Maybe those live bullets will change their attitudes a little.

March 12, 1966

I'm tired of waiting. Sometimes I wish they'd march us onto a boat or a plane for Vietnam, or wherever the hell we're going, so we could get it over with. I'm beginning to wonder whether I'll be walking around this time next year or not. And that ain't good. In action we probably won't have so much time to think about it. Up until now life has been so sweet. It's a little frightening sometimes to try and dig the future. Oh hell, screw it. Everybody goes when their wagon comes. I just hope mine is a long time coming.

On Dec. 16, 1966, Parks's company boarded ship and on Jan. 3, 1967, anchored off the coast of Vietnam.

January 31, 1967

The FO's job [Forward Observer] is one of the hairiest in a mortar platoon. He's on more patrols because an FO is required to be with the patrolling squad at all times, and there are only three FOs to cover sixteen squads. The odds are against him. Sgt. Paulson hand-picks the men for this job. So far he's fingered only Negroes and Puerto Ricans. I think he's trying to tell us something. I do know he gives me a sour look every time he sees me at the FDC [Fire Direction Control] controls. Every time he comes around I get a feeling that I should have been born white. It's a bitch. If only the souls and Puerto Ricans could tell the world what really happens to them in this man's army. We do receive more than our share of the shit.

February 2, 1967

The biggest laugh I've had lately was when I was on radio watch the other night and Paulson thought he'd sneak up on the radio tent and catch me napping. I heard a grunt and thud and looked out to see Paulson spread-eagled on the ground. I knew just what he'd been up to and burst out laughing. I really cracked up. Paulson was so ticked off all he did was get up and walk away. Paulson is a real ass. He's always telling me that Negroes are lazy and won't help themselves, etc. I tell him he's full of shit and end up filling sandbags.

Whitey is the same throughout this whole damn organization. Somehow I thought it would be different this time. Especially over here, where survival is the thing. But that seems to cut no ice with Mister Pale. All the souls in the platoon are beginning to gripe, but not enough as far as I'm concerned. Lt. Alden, the platoon leader, usually calls us Negroes "you people." Zerman, a Jewish cat from New York, is hip to what is happening, but he's got his own problems. Sgt. Golas changes with the weather. Sometimes he's human. At other times he treats us souls like we are dirt. What the hell. Maybe it's the pressure.

Ten more months of this crap. These guys bug me more than Charlie. I'm learning one hell of a lesson in here. Whitey's a good teacher.

February 7, 1967

The handwriting is definitely on the wall. Paulson says I'm not figuring the FDC data fast enough. Getting my walking boots ready.

May 5, 1967

Just heard from Deedee. She says Dad is still trying to get me into RIT [Rochester Institute of Technology]. He lectured up there once and they gave him some kind of an award, so maybe he's got influence. Good school. I've asked Deedee to help. Dad's a little slow on such things. Have to send her all the info for the admissions office.

May 8, 1967

In the hospital again. Same old jazz—the shrapnel wound in the bean department. A big lump keeps forming and they keep lancing it. God, some of the things you see here. One guy came in so badly shot up he tried to kill himself with a knife. I held him down while the medic put him out with a needle. An ARVN came in this morning with a foot blown off, dripping blood all over the floor. He didn't say anything or cry out. Probably just wondering where he would get another foot. Hope I don't have to go through anything like that.

The rains have started. Nothing but rain for the next four months, they say. My company is with the engineers building a temporary base on the Plain of Reeds. Everything out there is under water. After that we'll be on security and patrols.

May 15, 1967

Lot of thinking lately—the people I love, war, sex and what have you. Frankly I'm mixed up. The Stateside news bugs me. On the one hand you have Stokely Carmichael saying Negroes shouldn't be fighting for this country. On the other hand some Negro leaders think just the opposite. I doubt that most of them have ever been to war. One thing's for sure: I have been, and I'm fed up with it. This war is pointing up a lot of my mistakes. It's like the old man kept on telling me, "Champ, it looks like you're going to have to learn the hard way." If I get out of here in one piece, I'm going to be a different man. If you want to get something out of life, you're going to have to grab it and hold on to it. When I was in school before, I didn't realize this. I'm greedy now and don't think anything will step in my way.

Hope to be back with the fellows tomorrow.

May 17, 1967

Back with the company. It's hot and we're moving again toward another operation which starts tomorrow. I don't know where. They will probably deadline our tracks because of the mud. The jeeps can hardly make it on the roads. I never knew rain could be so troublesome.

Guys have been coming and going so fast it's hard to know anyone any more. Some of our guys are being transferred out to other units like the 273rd Infantry, and we get some of their men. The 273rd came over five months after our division, and the exchange will prevent our unit from being depleted when our one-year tour of duty is up. I won't be going since I've been transferred once. Twice is against the rules.

May 25, 1967

Rain has brought everything to a standstill, and Bravo is under about ten feet of water. Sometimes I would prefer action to sitting around listening to these officers beat their gums. It's either how many battles they've won or how many broads they've laid. At times they act like children the way they demand attention. And you'd better jump if you don't want your ass out on that firing line. The only way to keep cool with them is to lie quiet. Show the slightest sign of intelligence and you've had it. Especially if you're a Negro. Pratt and Gurney are pretty bright souls. But every time you see them they are pulling a shit detail while the white cats lie in their bunks enjoying life. A couple of the white guys got so ashamed that they came to the old man today and complained about Pratt and Gurney getting all the shit. I hope it does some good, but I doubt it.

Sgt. Paulson is detail boss. Capt. Thomas is a good officer and most of the time he treats me OK, probably because I'm his RTO [Radio Telephone Operator]. But sometimes he forgets himself. I made the mistake of showing him a clipping Deedee sent about Martin Luther King's denouncing the war. "Who the hell does he think he is? Just because he got a Nobel Prize he thinks he can run the fucking world." He went on, ripping King apart. I said that I thought Dr. King was a man who believed in justice for all people. Then I shut my big mouth. I wasn't in the mood for a night patrol.

17

"When the Black G.I.
Comes Home from Vietnam"

by Sol Stern

If lack of skills and education drive young blacks to the army in the first place, the military system could turn out to be a contributor to social equality in civilian life. By providing vocational training that blacks would otherwise not receive, the army could send back men qualified for jobs and reduce the number of hard corps unemployed.

On the other hand, the military teaches men to lead in combat situations. If ghetto conditions do not improve, if equal opportunity is not forthcoming, the black ex-soldiers provide excellent material for combat leadership in the cities.

Sol Stern was assistant managing editor of Ramparts *magazine when he discussed these issues in an article which appeared in* The New York Times *on March 24, 1968.*

In Vietnam, Charles Cato was a "tunnel rat"—a combat specialty reserved for the very small, the very agile and the very daring. He had to crawl through dark, narrow tunnels which may or may not have been sheltering armed Vietcong. One of several thousand black combat veterans now returning to the urban ghetto, Cato doesn't see anything extraordinary in what he did. "I didn't mind," he says. "I liked the job. I found it exciting."

Cato didn't come back to his old neighborhood in Bedford-Stuyvesant as a hero. No brass bands greet returning Vietnam veterans anywhere these days. In the black ghetto the main reaction to Cato's Vietnam experience has been some good-natured kidding from guys on the block for fighting "the white man's war."

Charley Cato wasn't exactly happy about going off to Vietnam. He was enjoying his freedom when he received his induction notice in 1965. Although he made only $55 per week as a jeweler's apprentice he liked his job and he felt he was learning a good trade. "I guess I just had to go though and so I went," he says quietly.

Trained as a rifleman and shipped to the 25th Infantry Division in Vietnam, Cato spent 12 months in the field around Pleiku, near the Cambodian border, and Chulai. He never even saw Saigon. Lots of his buddies were killed and wounded, and he did his own share of killing. He figures that he accounted for at least 11 Vietcong.

Charles Cato doesn't have much to show for his year under fire. He's living back home with his mother, brother and sister on a dreary, littered street in a battered four-story red-brick tenement house. His mother is on welfare. Cato was discharged from the Army three months ago but hasn't been able to find a job. His old job, as a jeweler's helper, isn't available. "Things are slow now," says his former boss. Cato is collecting $33 a week in unemployment insurance.

In Vietnam, he didn't give much thought to the rights or wrongs of the war. "I was just trying to stay alive and do my job," he says. How does he feel about it now? "I don't think that country was worth fighting for. But they told us we had to be there to stop Communism. I think now that we're in it we ought to win the war. We could win it if we wanted to. I know my buddies who died over there would have felt real bad if we don't win it now."

But Cato isn't bitter. He doesn't feel he has fought "the white man's war," and he doesn't have much sympathy for black militants. "I don't want to make any trouble. I don't feel I ought to hate whitey. A lot of my friends in Vietnam were white and we had good times together. I'm not prejudiced against white people."

David Tuck, a 26-year-old black veteran, returned from Vietnam and got back his old job with the Post Office—but he's still angry as hell. He's angry about the war, about the role that blacks have played in it and about the society he has come home to.

Tuck, from Cleveland's black ghetto, was drafted after he had dropped out of junior college at just about the same time that Charles Cato was drafted in Bedford-Stuyvesant. Tuck was also in the 25th Infantry Division and spent most of a year in Vietnam's central highlands as a radio-telephone operator, calling in artillery rounds.

Discharged from the service, he was so upset at what he had seen in Vietnam that he took the extraordinary step (for a young ex-G.I. with a Government job) of going to Copenhagen last December to give testimony at the Bertrand Russell International War Crimes Tribunal. He told the tribunal that he had witnessed atrocities committed against prisoners by American and South Vietnamese troops, including the beheading of a captured North Vietnamese by a G.I. in his own unit.

Tuck says that he went to Vietnam reluctantly. He had misgivings about the war but thought of it "as a mistake." After more reading and thinking about the war since returning he now says, "I realized this was really an imperialist country. In certain respects it was also a racial war. This country uses its minorities to do its dirty work up front in Vietnam—Negroes, Puerto Ricans and hillbillies. I think it's deliberate. These groups are the same ones that are most despised in American society and who nobody will miss."

Tuck acknowledges that in some respects Army life offers something to the Negro. "Ironically," he says, "I have to admit I found more democracy among enlisted men in the Army than outside. But this is the only freedom that black people have—to fight and die. Some black soldiers I know are re-enlisting, but that shows how bad the society is for black people—that they should have to stay in the Army to find a decent life."

Since returning from Vietnam, Tuck has become an activist in the Black Anti-Draft Union in Cleveland, encouraging other blacks to resist the draft by any means they can.

"I would never fight on a foreign shore for America again," says Tuck. "The only place I would fight is right here. Black people should not be called on to assume the duties of citizenship when they don't enjoy the rights and privileges. If a black man has the courage to fight 10,000 miles away he should have the courage to fight here. He could be killed as easily by a white man here as by a yellow man over there.

"A lot of black soldiers have been brainwashed. But when they come back and see that what they fought for doesn't mean a thing and that they are still considered niggers, well then, a lot of things are going to happen. It all depends on how much combat fatigue they have."

The sharp difference in the attitudes of these two

young ghetto blacks illustrates the variable effects of military experience on black consciousness. About 41,000 black veterans will be returning to civilian life this year [1968], and it is a reasonable guess that at least 5,000 will have served in Vietnam. No one person can speak for them and no opinion survey will ferret out their deepest feelings about the racial violence sweeping our cities. If they are inclined to take part in ghetto uprisings, using the skills they were taught by Uncle Sam, it is not the kind of thing they are likely to talk to an interviewer about. If there is one thing they have learned in the service it is how to play it cool. More likely than not, however, they don't yet know themselves how they will react if violence breaks out in their ghetto this summer.

To the ghetto militant, the returning black Viet vet is a potential source of leadership and tactical know-how in helping the black community organize for what they expect to be a savage summer of military repression. To the traditional civil-rights leadership, the returning vet could be a bastion of stability and moderation in the black community. To the jittery Defense Department official, the returning black G.I. is both a challenge and a threat. He is a potential, and potentially lethal, opponent who has to be neutralized by getting him off the ghetto streets, or he may be an ally, newly recruited into an urban police department to help with this summer's outbreaks.

To many blacks the military is the only way of escaping from the ghetto. If there are still remnants of discrimination and racism in the military it is also the only major institution in American society that has had a thorough going integration (even though black and white G.I.'s have engaged in racial brawls in the bars of Saigon and Danang). The extraordinary rate of black re-enlistment attests to this. In 1966, at a time when Vietnam casualties had started to mount dramatically, 60.5 per cent of Negroes in the Army on first term enlistments decided to re-enlist—a rate more than three times as high as that among whites.

The proverbial catch is that the Army also exacts a disproportionate price in blood for such benefits as it bestows. In Vietnam between 1961 and 1966, Negroes accounted for more than 20 per cent of Army fatalities even though they represented only 12.6 per cent of Army personnel in Vietnam.

Simply stated, the statistics show that the Negro in the Army was more likely than his white buddy to be sent to Vietnam in the first place; once there, was more likely to wind up in a front-line combat unit, and within the combat unit was more likely than the white to be killed or wounded.

The Defense Department explains the disparity by citing the high re-enlistment rate which tends to concentrate many Negroes in the exposed ranks of noncommissioned officers in combat units. Negroes also tend to volunteer for élite combat units such as the Airborne, says the department, because of the higher pay rates.

Yet another factor is that the Negro is more likely to be assigned to a combat unit during his first enlistment because of the lack of skills and education that drove him into the service in the first place. It is also quite likely that the black is presumed, *prima facie,* to be an unskilled young man, good mainly for infantry specialties, by those who make such assignments.

The popular motion-picture image of the black serviceman in World War II (and to some extent even in the Korean war) as the smiling, compliant cook, or supply handler in a segregated unit has thus radically altered. The black soldier has not only participated in his share of White House medal ceremonies and been featured on the covers of magazines, but he has been publicly praised for his contributions and heroism by General Westmoreland before the all-white Legislature of South Carolina.

But is the black man's new role in the military a gain or a tragedy that will ultimately breed more racial discord?

Lieut. Col. George Shoffer, one of the highest ranking Negro officers in the United States Army, sees it as a constructive development and a source of great personal pride. Schoffer spent almost a year of hard fighting in Vietnam as a commanding officer in the field, and led an all-black segregated unit in World War II.

When asked about the high casualty rate among Negroes in Vietnam, he said, "I feel good about it. Not that I like the bloodshed but the performance of the Negro in Vietnam tends to offset the fact that the Negro wasn't considered worthy of being a front-line soldier in other wars."

To the Negro militant, however, there is no pride in the combat performance of Negroes in Vietnam. Rather it is another in the long history of cruel jokes played upon the black man in white America—the black man is being forced to serve as cannon fodder for a war directed by whites against a colored people. Stokely Carmichael has said it is "clear that the [white] man is moving to get rid of black people in the ghettoes." . . .

In a 1966 article in *The New Republic*, Daniel Moynihan, former Assistant Secretary of Labor in the Kennedy and Johnson Administrations and one of the leading strategists of both Administrations' domestic programs, looked to the military as the only reasonable hope for America's disadvantaged poor—white and black alike.

Putting the issue bluntly, he said: "Civil rights as an issue is fading. The poverty program is heading for dismemberment and decline. Expectations of what can be done in America are receding. Very possibly our best hope is seriously to use the armed forces as a socializing experience for the poor—until somehow their environment begins turning out equal citizens."

Recognizing that the increased presence of Negroes in the armed services would also mean more blacks being shot at, Moynihan felt even this macabre corollary could be a civil-rights plus factor. "History may record," he wrote, "that the single most important psychological event in race relations in the nineteen-sixties was the appearance of Negro fighting men on the TV screens of the nation. Acquiring a reputation for military valor is one of the oldest known routes to social equality—from the Catholic Irish in the Mexican War to the Japanese-American Purple Heart Division of World War II."

Programs based on Mr. Moynihan's social analysis rest ultimately on certain blithe assumptions. First, there is the assumption that as whites in this society become aware of the valor and achievements of the Negro soldier their attitudes toward black people in general will change as it did toward other ethnic minorities in the past. But it is just those earlier ethnic minorities who are now the strongest sources of racism in the urban centers. If these and other whites were capable of seeing blacks as just another ethnic group there would be no race crisis.

More important, there is the assumption that a two- or three-year stint in the Army for the disadvantaged black will furnish him with useful skills and training. But given the present distribution of jobs in the armed services and the increasing pressures for more men in Vietnam, the low-income and poorly educated blacks inducted under

Project 100,000 are likely to leave the service having learned only how to march and fight.*

The new policy of drafting college graduates *en masse* may have the effect of reducing the over-all percentage of black participation in the armed services but it is also likely to increase the statistical imbalance of blacks assigned to combat specialties, since the new college-educated inductees, predominantly white, will tend to monopolize the skilled specialties.

Project 100,000 statistics show that among the "salvaged" blacks going into the Army, 42 per cent were assigned to the category of "Infantry, Gun Crews and Allied Specialties" as against 31.5 per cent of the white group. In the Marine Corps, 83.7 per cent of the blacks and 77.1 per cent of the whites in the "salvage" group were being assigned to combat specialties.

Thus a program touted for "developing a more stable society" and as a last "best hope" for civil rights may have effects which, in Pentagonese, could be called "counterproductive." You take a poorly educated, poorly motivated young Negro and put him through the harsh discipline of a highly integrated, competitive experience without teaching him useful occupational skills. You put him through a horrendous war, in which he cannot help but become conscious of the contributions and sacrifices his race is making, and then return him to civilian society

* Project 100,000, launched during the Johnson Administration, set as its goal the annual induction of 100,000 men previously rejected by the draft. Drawn largely from disadvantaged minority groups, they were to be given the educational and vocational opportunities they would not ordinarily have received in civilian life. Statistics for the first year starting October, 1966, show that almost forty percent of those men taken in were black. And the percentage assigned to combat specialties in this group was even higher than the already high rate among black men who had enlisted. [Editors' note.]

more disciplined, more competitive and with greater expectations for himself but with no specific talents he can sell—a society, furthermore, that has become in the interim, more polarized along racial lines. Under such conditions, some returning black Vietnam vets may become "destabilizing" elements rather than a force for civil-rights progress.

That is why militant black ghetto organizers such as Carlos Russell, who emerged as the leader of the black caucus at the Chicago New Politics Convention, look with some expectation to the returning black veteran. "The establishment will do everything to neutralize them, to see that they are not part of the movement. White America will do everything to make them turn their backs on their black brothers, but it won't work. They have been trained to kill; if rebellions break out and they see their black brothers and sisters slaughtered by racist cops they will come to the defense of their own. They offer a good resource of skills and technical know-how to those in the movement who feel the only solution is armed struggle." . . .

The New York regional veterans office [of the Urban League] is staffed by Otillo Mighty, a former Air Force sergeant with 20 years' service. Mighty spends most of his time on the phone nagging personnel departments of businesses in the New York area about this or that returned black veteran. A short, soft-spoken man who remembers having to re-enlist in the Air Force because he could not find a job in civilian life, Mighty is in as good a position as anyone to gauge the attitudes of the returning black Vietnam veterans. He has seen hundreds of them just after their discharge. Most of them, he feels, are trying hard to forget what they have been through.

"The black veteran," he says, "is like a cross-section of black America. There are all kinds of guys. But most of them seem to be apolitical. Don't forget he is a guy who has been cut out of circulation and isolated for two years. And he has had very little time for anything like political stuff. I'm not saying they won't ever get involved. If some of the vets use what they have learned over there it won't really be surprising. On the other hand if a lot of others don't do anything I wouldn't be surprised either." . . .

Tired of fighting and killing, happy to be alive, wanting to forget what he has been through, trying to organize his civilian life, getting a good job, finishing his education, the black Viet vet is not likely to become a political activist immediately—as was the engaged white veteran of World War II. He is probably still confused about the meaning of his experience in Vietnam. He is not getting involved in anti-Vietnam war groups. Of the 200 or so Vietnam vets who have associated themselves with a group called Vietnam Veterans Against the War, only a handful have been black.

The case of Bill Robinson is probably typical. He is a 21-year-old vet just returned home to the Bronx after five months in an artillery unit in Vietnam. Within a few days of his discharge, Mr. Mighty at the Urban League helped him get a $7,500-a-year job as an account executive with a Manhattan dry-cleaning firm. Robinson isn't joining any groups nor has he been approached by any organizers. He wants to forget what he saw in Vietnam. He's grateful for the help he got from the Urban League and recognizes that his status as a vet is helping him financially, but he isn't any less conscious of the race question and he isn't suddenly in love with the Great Society.

"A black G.I. coming back from Vietnam can't help

feeling strongly about the situation here," he says. "Don't be deceived that just because he gets a job that he isn't going to get involved. The important thing is that he's coming back to the same old stuff. Just helping a man get a job isn't going to erase the bitterness and the sense of injustice. It is a step in the right direction but it isn't the answer."

Robinson believes that, having experienced warfare, the black G.I. is not looking for more of it here at home in the cities, but being acclimated to violence he will not run from it either if and when his people are its victims.

This view is shared by Don Ferguson, a 23-year-old black veteran of Vietnam, now looking for a job in New York City. Ferguson joined the Marines three years ago "to get off the streets. In the service you are taught the other man is trying to kill you and you have to kill him first," says Ferguson. "You learn self-preservation—wrong or right doesn't matter much. And veterans are going to react that way. I feel that if there are riots this summer there will be a lot of vets fighting. If it comes to them they will react."

On the basis of conversations with a dozen returned black veterans one might hazard these generalizations that having fought and lived alongside white in an integrated Army and having probably gotten some economic benefits from having served, they are more than ever aware of the deep racial gulf that separates them from mainstream America. If, to the disappointment of some ghetto militants, they are not yet stashing away M-14's for the day of reckoning, many of them will still move with the tide of militancy and nationalism now rising in the ghetto. Under appropriate conditions some will be ready to resort to guns.

How many will move in that direction no one can say.

In one sense, numbers do not matter much. There is still one black man reenlisting for another tour of military service for every one who is discharged—and many of those who re-enlist wind up in units such as the 82d Airborne, used during the uprising in Detroit last summer to suppress other blacks. If, as the black militants are saying, when racial conflict reaches the peak there will be open season on all blacks, then that black G.I. who remained in the 82d Airborne may become an even greater threat than the black ex-G.I. in the ghetto. Under those conditions he may feel he is black first and soldier second, and turn his gun around.

Ultimately, it is extremely dangerous to try to use the military to solve social problems in a society that is torn by racial conflict. It is a dangerous illusion to think that under such conditions the experience of white and black young men fighting and dying together overseas could have a cleansing effect. The military experience is a very special one; when it is over there is an entirely different ball game to go home to. David Parks understood this when he sensed that the man who was willing to share a canteen with him when both were thrown together and trying to survive in the mud in Vietnam wouldn't have lunch with him back in his clean, peaceful hometown.

A society that feeds millions of its disadvantaged young men into the military machine in the name of "civil rights" may only insure that when social conflict reaches its violent climax, it will be fought on both sides with greater military sophistication and more lethal weapons and by young men grown accustomed to killing.

18

"From Dakto to Detroit: Death of a Troubled Hero"

by Jon Nordheimer

from *The New York Times*, May 25, 1971

This is the story of a black soldier who won the Congressional Medal of Honor in Vietnam, and died of gunshot wounds in Detroit. It is the painful account of a man who found that a black G.I. had trouble getting a job, but a black Medal of Honor winner did not. And it seems to be the tragedy of a man whose conscience rebelled at the idea of making a meal ticket out of membership in the Congressional Medal of Honor Society.

We will probably never know exactly what motivated Sergeant Dwight Johnson to rob the grocery store near his home, but as correspondent Jon Nordheimer makes abundantly clear, it had a great deal to do with being a black soldier.

A few tenants living in the E. J. Jefferies Homes, a dreary public housing project in Corktown, an old Detroit neighborhood, can still remember Dwight Johnson as a little boy who lived in one of the rust-brown buildings with his mother and baby brother. They think it strange, after all that has happened to Dwight, to remember him as a gentle boy who hated to fight.

Dwight Johnson died one week from his 24th birthday, shot and killed as he tried to rob a grocery store a mile from his home. The store manager later told the police that a tall Negro had walked in shortly before midnight, drawn a revolver out of his topcoat and demanded money from the cash register.

The manager pulled his own pistol from under the counter and the two men struggled. Seven shots were fired.

Four and one-half hours later, on an operating table at Detroit General Hospital, Dwight (Skip) Johnson died from five gunshot wounds.

Ordinarily, the case would have been closed right there, a routine crime in a city where there were 13,583 armed robberies last year.

But when the detectives went through the dead man's wallet for identification, they found a small white card with its edges rubbed thin from wear. "Congressional Medal of Honor Society—United States of America," it said. "This certifies that Dwight H. Johnson is a member of this society."

The news of the death of Sgt. Dwight Johnson shocked the black community of Detroit. Born out of wedlock when his mother was a teenager and raised on public welfare, he had been the good boy on his block in the dreary housing project, an altar boy and Explorer Scout, one of the few among the thousands of poor black youngsters in Detroit who had struggled against the grinding life of the ghetto and broken free, coming home from Vietnam tall and strong and a hero.

The story of Dwight Johnson and his drift from hero in Dakto, Vietnam, to villain in Detroit is a difficult one to trace. The moments of revelation are rare. There were, of course, those two brief episodes that fixed public attention on him: 30 minutes of "uncommon valor" one cold morning in combat that earned him the nation's highest military decoration, and the 30-second confrontation in the Detroit grocery that ended his life.

Oddly, they are moments of extreme violence, and everyone who knew Dwight Johnson—or thought he did—knew he was not a violent man.

Now that the funeral is over and the out-of-town relatives have gone home and the family conferences that sought clues to explain Dwight's odd behavior have ended in bitter confusion, his mother can sit back and talk wistfully about the days when Skip was a skinny kid who was chased home after school by the Corktown bullies.

"Mama," he would ask, "what do I do if they catch me?" His mother would place an arm around his thin shoulders and draw him close. "Skip," she would say, "don't you fight, honey, and don't let them catch you." The boy would look downcast and worried. "Yes, Mama," he'd say.

"Dwight was a fabulous, all-around guy, bright and with a great sense of humor," reflected Barry Davis, an auburn-haired Californian who flew with his wife to Detroit when he heard on a news report that Dwight had been killed. Three others who had served with him in Vietnam, all of them white, also came, not understanding what aberration had led to his death.

"I can remember our first day at Fort Knox and Dwight was the only colored guy in our platoon," Barry Davis recalled. "So we're in formation and this wise guy from New Jersey says to Dwight, 'Hey, what's the initials N.A.A.C.P. stand for?'

"And Dwight says, 'The National Association for the Advancement of Colored People.'

"And this wise guy from New Jersey says, 'Naw, that ain't it. It stands for Niggers Acting As Colored People.'

"And I said to myself, 'Wow, those are fighting words,' but Dwight just laughed. From then on he was just one of the guys. As it turned out, Dwight liked this wise guy from New Jersey in the end as much as he liked anybody."

Most of the men who served with Sergeant Dwight Johnson remembered him that way—easy-going, hard to rattle, impossible to anger.

But Stan Enders remembers him another way. Stan was the gunner in Skip's tank that morning in Vietnam three years ago, during the fighting at Dakto.

"No one who was there could ever forget the sight of this guy taking on a whole battalion of North Vietnamese soldiers," Stan said as he stood in the sunshine outside Faith Memorial Church in Corktown three weeks ago, waiting for Skip's funeral service to begin.

Their platoon of four M-48 tanks was racing down a road toward Dakto, in the Central Highlands near the Cambodian border and the Ho Chi Minh Trail, when it was ambushed. Communist rockets knocked out two of the tanks immediately, and waves of foot soldiers sprang out of the nearby woods to attack the two tanks still in commission.

Skip hoisted himself out of the turret hatch and manned the mounted .50-caliber machine gun. He had been assigned to this tank only the night before. His old tank, and the crew he had spent 11 months and 22 days with in Vietnam and had never seen action before, was 60 feet away, burning.

"He was really close to those guys in that tank," Stan said. "He just couldn't sit still and watch it burn with them inside."

Skip ran through heavy crossfire to the tank and opened its hatch. He pulled out the first man he came across in the turret, burned but still alive, and got him to the ground just as the tank's artillery shells exploded, killing everyone left inside.

"When the tank blew up and Dwight saw the bodies all burned and black, well, he just sort of cracked up," said Stan.

For 30 minutes, armed first with a .45-caliber pistol and then with a submachine gun, Skip hunted the Vietnamese on the ground, killing from five to 20 enemy soldiers, nobody knows for sure. When he ran out of ammunition, he killed one with the stock of the machine gun.

At one point he came face to face with a Communist soldier who squeezed the trigger on his weapon aimed point-blank at him. The gun misfired and Skip killed him. But the soldier would come back to haunt him late at night in Detroit, in those dreams in which that anonymous soldier stood in front of him, the barrel of his AK-47 as big as a railroad tunnel, his finger on the trigger, slowly pressing it.

"When it was all over," Stan said, walking up the church steps as the funeral service got under way, "it took three men and three shots of morphine to hold Dwight down. He was raving. He tried to kill the prisoners we had rounded up. They took him away to a hospital in Pleiku in a straightjacket."

Stan saw Skip the next day. He had been released from the hospital, and came by to pick up his personal gear. His Vietnam tour was over and he was going home.

No one there would know anything about Dakto until 10 months later, at the White House Medal of Honor ceremony.

Sergeant Johnson returned home in early 1968, outwardly only little changed from the quiet boy named Skip who had grown up in Detroit and been drafted. Even when he and the other black veterans came home and could not find a job, he seemed to take it in stride.

He had been discharged with $600 in his pocket, and it was enough to buy cigarettes and go out at night with his cousin, Tommy Tillman, and with Eddie Wright, a friend from the Jefferies Homes, and make the rounds to the Shadowbox or the Little Egypt, to drink a little beer and have a few dates.

And at home no one knew about the bad dreams he was having. They would have to learn about that later from an Army psychiatrist.

If anyone asked him about Vietnam he would just shake his head, or laugh and say, "Aw, man, nothing happened," and he would change the subject and talk about the girls in Kuala Lumpur where he went for R & R, or the three-day pass he spent in Louisville, Ky., drinking too much whisky for the first time in his life and ending up in jail.

He returned home just as the Communist Tet offensive erupted in Vietnam, and everyone talked about how lucky he had been to get out before things got hot. They teased him then about his lackluster military career.

"When he came home from Vietnam he was different, sure. I noticed it, all jumpy and nervous and he had to be doing something all the time, it seems," said Eddie Wright. "But mostly he was the same fun-time guy."

Carmen Berry, a close friend of Katrina May, the girl

Skip started dating after his discharge, thought she detected nuances of change she attributed to the same mental letdown she had seen in other Vietnam veterans.

"They get quiet," she said. "It's like they don't have too much to say about what it was like over there. Maybe it's because they've killed people and they don't really know why they killed them."

"The only thing that bugged me about Skip then," reflected his cousin Tommy, "and the one thing I thought was kind of strange and unlike him, was the pictures he brought back. He had a stack of pictures of dead people, you know, dead Vietnamese. Color slides."

In the fall he started looking for a job, along with Tommy Tillman.

"We'd go down to the state employment agency every day and take a look at what was listed," his cousin recalled. "Skip was funny; he wouldn't try for any of the hard jobs. If we wrote down the name of a company that had a job that he didn't feel qualified for, he wouldn't even go into the place to ask about it. He'd just sit in the car while I went in.

"Or if he did go in some place, he'd just sit and mumble a few words when they'd ask him questions. It was like he felt inferior. He'd give a terrible impression. But once we got back in the car, it was the same old Skip, laughing and joking."

One day in October two military policemen came to his house. His mother saw the uniforms and before opening the door whispered urgently, "What did you do?"

"I didn't do nothing, honest, Ma," he answered.

The M.P.s asked Skip a few questions. They wanted to know what he was doing and if he had been arrested since his discharge. Fifteen minutes after they left, the telephone rang. It was a colonel, calling from the Department of Defense in Washington. Sergeant Johnson was being awarded the Medal of Honor, he said. Could he and his family be in Washington on Nov. 19 so President Johnson could personally present the award?

One week later, on Nov. 19, 1968, they were all there in the White House, Skip tall and handsome in his dress-blue uniform, his mother, Katrina and Tommy Tillman. The President gave a little speech. The national election was over, the Democrats had lost, but there were signs of movement at the Paris peace talks.

"Our hearts and our hopes are turned to peace as we assemble here in the East Room this morning," the President said. *"All our efforts are being bent in its pursuit. But in this company we hear again, in our minds, the sound of distant battles."*

Five men received the Medal of Honor that morning. And when Sergeant Johnson stepped stiffly forward and the President looped the pale blue ribbon and sunburst medal around his neck, a citation was read that described his valor.

Later, in the receiving line, when his mother reached Skip she saw tears streaming down his face.

"Honey," she whispered, "what are you crying about? You've made it back."

After he officially became a hero, it seemed that everyone in Detroit wanted to hire Dwight Johnson, the only living Medal of Honor winner in Michigan. Companies that had not been interested in a diffident ex-G.I. named Johnson suddenly found openings for Medal of Honor Winner Johnson.

Among those who wanted him was the United States Army.

"The brass wanted him in the Detroit recruiting office because—let's face it—here was a black Medal of Honor winner, and blacks are our biggest manpower pool in Detroit," said an Army employe who had worked with Skip after he rejoined the service a month after winning the medal. "Personally, I think a lot of promises were made to the guy that couldn't be kept. You got to remember that getting this guy back into the Army was a feather in the cap of a lot of people.

Events began moving quickly then for Skip. He married Katrina in January (the Pontchartrain Hotel gave the couple its bridal suite for their wedding night), and the newlyweds went to Washington in January as guests at the Nixon inaugural. Sergeant Johnson began a long series of personal appearances across Michigan in a public relations campaign mapped by the Army.

In February, 1,500 persons paid $10 a plate to attend a testimonial dinner for the hero in Detroit's Cobo Hall, co-sponsored by the Ford Motor Company and the Chamber of Commerce. A special guest was Gen. William C. Westmoreland, Army Chief of Staff and former commander of United States forces in Vietnam.

"Dwight was a hot property back in those days," recalled Charles Bielak, a civilian information officer for the Army's recruiting operations in Detroit. "I was getting calls for him all over the state. Of course, all this clamor didn't last. It reached a saturation point somewhere along the way and tapered off."

But while it lasted, Skip's life was frenetic. Lions Clubs . . . Rotary . . . American Legion. Detroit had a new hero. Tiger Stadium and meet the players. Sit at the dais with the white politicians. Be hailed by the black businessmen who would not have bothered to shake his hand before. Learn which fork to use for the salad. Say something intelligent to the reporters. Pick up the check for dinner for friends. Live like a man who had it made.

But Leroy May, the hero's father-in-law, could still see the child behind the man.

"Dwight and Katrina were a perfect match—they both had a lot of growing up to do," he said. "They didn't know how to handle all the attention they got in those early days. They'd go out to supper so much Katrina complained she couldn't eat any more steak. I had to take them out and buy them hot dogs and soda pop. They were just like a couple of kids."

Bills started piling up. "They were in over their heads as soon as they were married," Mr. May said.

Everyone extended credit to the Medal of Honor winner. Even when he bought the wedding ring, the jeweler would not take a down payment. Take money from a hero? Not then. Later, the Johnsons discovered credit cards.

At first they lived in an $85-a-month apartment. But Katrina wanted a house. Skip signed a mortgage on a $16,000 house on the west side of Detroit. Monthly payments were $160.

In the spring of 1970, he wrote a bad check for $41.77 at a local market. The check was made good by a black leader in Detroit who was aghast that the Medal of Honor winner had gotten himself into a financial hole.

"I went to see him and told him he couldn't go on like this," said the man, a lawyer who asked to remain anonymous. "I said he was young and black and had the Medal of Honor. He could do anything he wanted. I tried to get him to think about college and law school. The black businessmen would pick up the tab. He wouldn't have any part of it."

Looking back on this meeting, the lawyer said he suspected Skip was burdened by a "ghetto mentality" that limited his horizons. His world had been a public housing project and schools a few blocks away. Now, suddenly, events had thrust him outside the security of his boyhood neighborhood into a world dominated by whites.

He was paralyzed, the lawyer speculated, by an inability to formulate a plan of action in this alien culture that he had been transported to by something that happened on the other side of the globe.

"What does he do when he's introduced to Bunkie Knudsen, the president of Ford?" asked the lawyer. "Does he come across strong and dynamic because he knows there is a $75,000-a-year job waiting for him if he makes a good impression? And what happens to him when he just stands there and fumbles and doesn't know if he should shake hands or just nod his head? He was forced to play a role he was never trained for and never anticipated."

Tommy Tillman remembers how Skip would take several friends downtown to the Pontchartrain Hotel for an expensive meal and sit fumbling with the silverware, watching the others to see what fork to use first. "I'd say to him, 'Shoot, man, what do you care? Go ahead and use anything you want.'

"I wondered how he must feel when he's the guest of honor at one of those fancy meetings he was all the time going to."

It was about this time that the stomach pains started.

"It was all that rich food he was eating," said his father-in-law. His mother recalled that "Skip always did have a nervous stomach."

He began staying away from his job as a recruiter, missed appointments and speaking engagements. "It got so I had to pick him up myself and deliver him to a public appearance," said Mr. Bielak. "I had to handcuff myself to the guy to get him someplace. It was embarrassing. I couldn't understand his attitude."

Last summer it was decided that Sergeant Johnson should report to Selfridge Air Force Base, not far from Detroit, for diagnosis of stomach complaints.

From Selfridge he was sent in September to Valley Forge Army Hospital in Pennsylvania. An Army psychiatrist later mulled over his notes on the patient and talked about them:

Maalox and bland diet prescribed. G.I. series conducted. Results negative. Subject given 30-day convalescent leave to 16 October 1970. Absent without leave until 21 January 1971 when subject returned to Army hospital on own volition. Subsequent hearing recommended dismissal of A.W.O.L. charge and back pay reinstated. Subject agreed to undergo psychiatric evaluation. In cognizance of subject's outstanding record in Vietnam, the division's chief psychiatrist placed in charge of the case. Preliminary analysis: Depression caused by post-Vietnam adjustment problem.

In February, Eddie Wright bumped into Skip on a Detroit street.

"Hey, man, where've you been?"

"I just got out of Valley Forge on a pass."

"How things going there?"

"They got me in the psycho ward."

"Huh, you got to be kidding."

"No, man, they think I'm crazy."

During the convalescent leave, Sergeant Johnson borrowed $4,992 from a Detroit credit union. In his wallet he had a cashier's check for $1,500, the back pay the Army had awarded him. Most of his time he spent at home on the pass but when he went out he would drive to the Jefferies Homes and play basketball with the teenagers after school.

"He was a big man down there with the kids," recalled his cousin. "We had all lived in the project and had been on welfare, just like those kids there today, and we were like heroes because we had broken out of there. We had made it to the outside world, and to them we were big successes. We had made it.

"Skip was something special. He had that medal, and they were proud of him. He'd be down there five minutes and the kids would come around and say, 'Hey man, ain't you Dwight Johnson?' "

His old high school crowd was concerned about some of his new friends, though. "They were strung out on drugs, and they just seemed to be hanging around Skip for his money," said his mother. "I asked him one night if he was taking anything, and he rolled up his sleeves and showed me there were no tracks [needle marks]. 'Ma,' he said, 'I'm not taking a thing.' "

On his return to the hospital, he began analysis with the chief attending psychiatrist.

Subject is bright. His Army G.T. rating is equivalent of 120 I.Q. In first interviews he does not volunteer information. He related he grew up in a Detroit ghetto and never knew his natural father. He sort of laughed when he said he was a "good boy" and did what was expected of him. The only time he can remember losing his temper as a youth was when neighborhood bullies picked on his younger brother. He was so incensed grownups had to drag him off the other boys. In general, there is evidence the subject learned to live up to the expectations of others while there was a build-up of anger he continually suppressed.

The Army hospital is actually in Phoenixville, Pa., several miles from Valley Forge. It is the principal treatment center for psychiatric and orthopedic patients in the Northeast, with 1,200 beds now occupied.

Because of the large number of amputees and wheelchair patients, the hospital has only two floors and is spread over several acres. Long oak-floored corridors run in all directions, connected by covered walkways and arcades. Someone once measured the hospital and found there were seven miles of corridors in a maze-like jumble. To prevent patients from losing their way, wards are painted different colors.

Dressed in hospital blue denims, the warrior-hero walked the labyrinth late at night, wrestling with the problems that tormented his mind and drained his spirit.

"The first day Dwight arrived here, the hospital's sergeant major brought him to us," said Spec. 6 Herman Avery, a tall Negro with a flat face and close-set eyes, who was master of the ward Dwight was first assigned to at the hospital. "It was the first time the sergeant major ever did that. We got the message. This guy was something special.

"Well, practically the first night he's here they dress him up and take him over to the Freedoms Foundations in Valley Forge to shake hands. When he got back he told me that if they ever did that again he would go A.W.O.L."

There was further psychiatric evaluation.

Subject expressed doubts over his decision to re-enter the Army as a recruiter. He felt the Army didn't honor

242   THE BLACK SOLDIER

*its commitment to him. The public affairs were satisfac-
tory to him at first, but he started to feel inadequate.
People he would meet would pump his hand and slap his
back and say, "Johnson, if you ever think about getting
out of the Army, come look me up." On several occasions
he contacted these individuals and they didn't remember
him. It always took several minutes to remind them who
he was.*

Back in Detroit on leave on one occasion, his mother
asked him to drive her to a doctor's appointment. In
the office, an off-duty black Detroit policeman, Ronald
Turner, recognized the Medal of Honor winner. When
he asked for an account of his experience in Vietnam,
Skip replied: "Don't ask me anything about the medal. I
don't even know how I won it."

Later, the policeman reported Skip complained that he
had been exploited by the Army. He told him that ever
since he won the medal he had been set on a hero's path
as an inspiration to black kids.

Others recalled how upset he had become when his
recruiting talks at some black high schools in Detroit had
been picketed by militants who called him an "electronic
nigger," a robot the Army was using to recruit blacks for
a war in Asia.

With his psychiatrist, he began to discuss his deeper
anxieties.

*Since coming home from Vietnam the subject has had
bad dreams. He didn't confide in his mother or wife, but
entertained a lot of moral judgment as to what had happened at Dakto. Why had he been ordered to switch tanks
the night before? Why was he spared and not the others?*

He experienced guilt about his survival. He wondered if he was sane. It made him sad and depressed.

Skip signed out of the hospital on March 28 on a three-day pass to Philadelphia. The next day the newspapers and television were filled with reports of the conviction of First Lieut. William L. Calley Jr. on charges of murdering Vietnamese civilians. Skip turned up in Detroit a few days later and never returned to the Army hospital.

He settled in at home once again and dodged the telephone calls from the Army.

"How can you take punitive action against a Medal of Honor holder?" asked a major at the hospital who tried to convince him to return.

The Army did contact the Ford Motor Company, however, which had been letting Skip use a Thunderbird for the past two years. Ford picked up the car on the theory that without it he might be inconvenienced enough to return to the hospital. Instead, he cashed the cashier's check for $1,500, his Army back pay, and bought a 1967 Mercury for $850. He changed his unlisted phone number to avoid the Army callers and a growing number of bill collectors.

By April, his house mortgage had not been paid for the previous nine months, and foreclosing proceedings had been started. He owed payments on his credit union loan.

The car had to go into a garage for brake repairs on Wednesday, April 28, and Skip was told it would cost $78.50 to get it out. The same day, Katrina entered a hospital for removal of an infected cyst, and he told the admitting office clerk he would pay the $25 deposit the next day.

Lonely and depressed at home, Skip telephoned his cousin. "Let's go out and grab some beers," he said. But his cousin was busy.

He made another phone call that night and spoke to a friend in the Army. "I have a story I'm writing and I want you to peddle it for me," he said. "It starts out like this:

"Sgt. Dwight Johnson is dead and his home has been wiped out. . . ."

On April 30, Skip visited Katrina at the hospital. She said they were asking about the hospital deposit. He left at 5:30, promising to return later that evening with her hair curlers and bathrobe.

"He was just the same old Dwight, just kidding and teasing," his wife recalled. "When he was going, he said, 'Ain't you going to give me a little kiss good-by?' He said it like a little boy with his thumb in his mouth. So I kissed him and he went."

When Eddie Wright got home from work that night about 9 o'clock, he got a call from Skip. He said he needed a ride to pick up some money someone owed him and wanted to know if Eddie could get his stepfather to drive him. He said he would pay $15 for the ride.

Around 11 o'clock, Eddie, his mother and his step-father picked up Skip at his home. At his direction they drove west for about a mile to the corner of Orangelawn and Prest.

"Stop here," Skip told him, getting out of the car. "This guy lives down the street and I don't want him to see me coming."

The family waited in the car for 30 minutes. They be-came nervous, parked in a white neighborhood, and as Eddie explained later to the police, it may have looked odd for a car filled with blacks to be parked on a dark street. "So we pulled the car out under a streetlight so everybody could see us," he said.

At about 11:45 a police car pulled up sharply and two officers with drawn pistols got out. "What are you doing here?" they asked.

"We're waiting for a friend."

"What's his name?"

"Dwight Johnson."

"Dwight Johnson's on the floor of a grocery store around the corner," the officers said. "He's been shot."

"I first hit him with two bullets," the manager, Charles Landeghem, said later. "But he just stood there, with the gun in his hand, and said, 'I'm going to kill you. . . .'

"I kept pulling the trigger until my gun was empty."

Skip's psychiatrist recalled one of the interviews with him.

The subject remembered coming face to face with a Vietnamese with a gun. He can remember the soldier squeezing the trigger. The gun jammed. The subject has since engaged in some magical thinking about this episode. He also suffers guilt over surviving it, and later winning a high honor for the one time in his life when he lost complete control of himself. He asked: "What would happen if I lost control of myself in Detroit and behaved like I did in Vietnam?" The prospect of such an event apparently was deeply disturbing to him.

The burial at Arlington National Cemetery took place on a muggy and overcast day. The grave, on a grassy slope about 200 yards east of the Kennedy Memorial, overlooks the Potomac and the Pentagon, gray and silent, to the south.

The Army honor guard, in dress blues, carried out its

assignment with precision, the sixth burial of the day for the eight-man unit, while tourists took photographs at a discreet distance from the grieving family.

For a few days after the burial, the family weighed the possibility that Skip had been taking narcotics in the last few months of his life and the demands of drugs had sent him into the grocery store with a gun. But the autopsy turned up no trace of narcotics.

Eddie Wright and his family were released by homicide detectives after questioning, even after Eddie could not produce any plausible reason why his best friend had carried out a bizarre crime and implicated him at the same time.

The dead man's mother was the only one who uttered the words that no one else dared to speak.

"Sometimes I wonder if Skip tired of this life and needed someone else to pull the trigger," she said late one night in the living room of her home, her eyes fixed on a large color photograph of her son, handsome in his uniform, with the pale blue ribbon of his country's highest military honor around his neck.

EPILOGUE

It is both ironic and tragic that a growing number of blacks are refusing service in the armed forces. It is ironic because, after seeking the privilege of serving for two hundred years, many blacks have decided it is not such a privilege after all. Instead, military duty at the front has taken on the aura of still another rejection. That is to say, at this time, when the war itself is in such a disfavor, it appears to some that by sending a disproportionate number of blacks into combat zones the army prefers to spare white lives at the expense of black. The tragedy is that many black youths do not feel that America is worth fighting for to begin with.

Some blacks feel strongly enough about discrimination at home to refuse induction altogether, whatever the consequences. A few find the issue a convenient excuse to dodge the draft, but others are truly committed to the pursuit of civil liberty. An example of this attitude is a man by the name of John Otis Sumrall. Sumrall was one of the first blacks to challenge the legality of segregated draft boards. He asked the court to forbid induction or classification of Negroes until the number of Negroes on draft boards was proportional to the local population. His suit also maintained that the Mississippi State Director of Selective Service had personally intervened to have three criminal charges against him dismissed, and that he was called out of turn for induction so as to terminate his civil rights activities. In August, 1967, he was sentenced to five years in prison and a $2,500 fine for refusing induction. Sumrall asked the question that an increasing number of young blacks are asking today: "If I am not looked upon as an equal citizen in everyday life, why am I looked upon as an equal citizen when it comes time for me to report for induction?" This is a fair question and one which must be answered satisfactorily if further black alienation is to be prevented.

On the other side of the coin, the armed forces, reflecting American society in general, have traditionally been a source of upward mobility, at least for the white population. It is possible, therefore, that the recent top promotions of black men in both the army and navy indicates a belated recognition of the importance of mobility and equality of opportunity within the services—and possibly, just possibly, a reflection of greater opportunity without.